TRAVELMATE

compiled by

LEXUS

RICHARD DREW PUBLISHING
Glasgow

RICHARD DREW PUBLISHING LTD.
20 PARK CIRCUS
GLASGOW G3 6BE
SCOTLAND

First Published 1982
First Reprint April 1982
Second Reprint May 1984
Third Reprint May 1985

ISBN 0 904002 74 8

Printed and bound in Great Britain by
Cox & Wyman Ltd.

YOUR TRAVELMATE gives you one single A–Z list of useful words and phrases to help you communicate in French. Built into this list are travel tips, with facts and figures which provide valuable information; French words you'll see on signs and notices; and typical replies to some of the things you might want to say. There is a menu reader on pp. 72–73, and numbers are given on the last page.

Your TRAVELMATE also tells you how to pronounce French. Just read the pronunciations as though they were English, and you will communicate – although you might not sound like a native speaker. The typical French nasal sounds are represented by [o͞n] and [a͞n]. [j] is like the second consonant sound in 'measure' or 'seizure'. Practice and listening to the French will soon help you distinguish between difficult sounds.

Depending on the likely context of use, the TRAVELMATE gives the French equivalent of either 'the' or 'a'. In some cases, you will also find 'du', 'de la' or plural 'des', for English 'some'. The feminine form of adjectives has not, as a rule, been given; remember that the final consonant is sounded in the feminine form: chaud, chaude [shoh, shoh**d**], creux, creuse [krer, krer**z**], certain, certaine [sair-ta͞n, sair-**ten**]

The present tense of verbs will be sufficient to help you get by in most situations:
arriver [ahree-**vay**] – j'arrive [jah-reev], tu arrives [too ah-reev], il (elle) arrive [eel, el ah-reev], nous arrivons [nooz ahree-**von**], vous arrivez [vooz ahree-**vay**], ils (elles) arrivent [eelz, elz ah-reev]

Finally, you may need to spell your name:
a [ah] b [bay] c [say] d [day] e [ay] f [eff] g [jay]
h [ash] i [ee] j [jee] k [kah] l [el] m [em] n [en] o [oh]
p [pay] q [koo] r [airr] s [ess] t [tay] u [oo] v [vay]
w [doobler vay] x [eeks] y [ee-grek] z [zed]

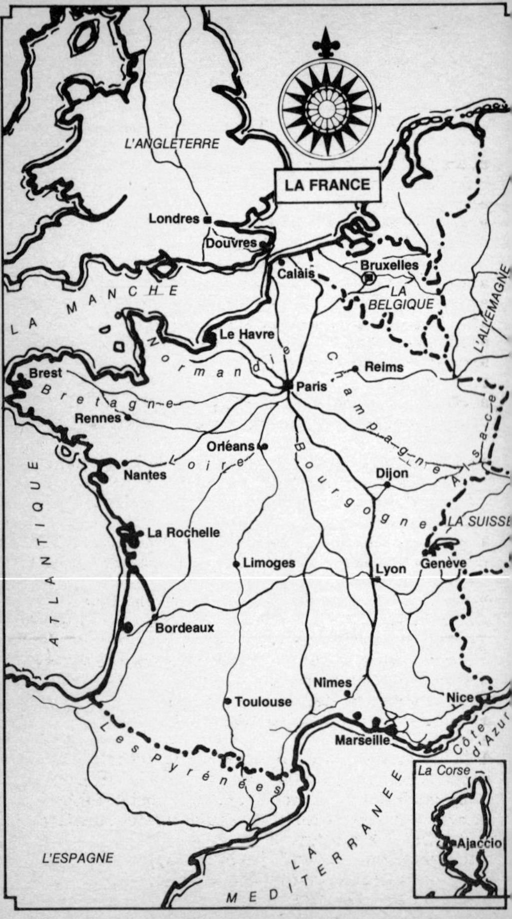
LA FRANCE
L'ANGLETERRE
Londres
Douvres
Calais
Bruxelles
LA BELGIQUE
L'ALLEMAGNE
LA MANCHE
Le Havre
Normandie
Champagne
Reims
Brest
Bretagne
Paris
Rennes
Orléans
Loire
Alsace
Nantes
Bourgogne
Dijon
ATLANTIQUE
La Rochelle
LA SUISSE
Limoges
Genève
Lyon
Bordeaux
Nîmes
Toulouse
Nice
Côte d'Azur
Marseille
Les Pyrénées
La Corse
Ajaccio
L'ESPAGNE
LA MEDITERRANEE

a, an un (une) [an, oon]
5 francs a litre cinq francs le litre [san fron ler leetr]
aboard à bord [ah-bor]
about: is he about? est-ce qu'il est là? [eskee-lay lah]
about 15 environ quinze [onvee-ron kanz]
about 2 o'clock vers deux heures [vair . . .]
above: au-dessus (de . . .) [oh der-soo]
abroad à l'étranger [ah laytron-jay]
absolutely absolument [apsoh-loo-mon]
accelerator l'accélérateur [axay-lay-rah-terr]
accept accepter [axep-tay]
accès interdit *no entry*
accident un accident [axee-don]
there's been an accident il y a eu un accident [eelyah oo . . .]
» *TRAVEL TIP: if anybody is hurt, get the police; for minor accidents, make sure both parties sign the 'constat à l'amiable' (forms provided with your green card documents)*
accommodation: we need accommodation for 3 il nous faut de la place pour trois personnes [eel noo foh der lah plass . . .]
» *TRAVEL TIP: go to the local 'syndicat d'initiative' (tourist office) for information; one- or two-star hotels are almost always a good bet; also 'gîtes ruraux' (self-catering accommodation) and 'gîtes d'étape' (dormitory accommodation for ramblers etc)*
accotements non stabilisés *soft verges*
accountant un comptable [kon-tahbl]
accurate précis
A.C.F. *= Automobile Club de France, like RAC*
ache: it aches c'est douloureux [say dooloo-rer]
my back aches j'ai mal au dos [jay maloh-doh]
across: across (the river) de l'autre côté (de la rivière) [der loht koh-tay der . . .]
to get across traverser [trahvair-say]
adaptor un adaptateur [ahdap-tah-terr]
add ajouter [ahjoo-tay]

address une adresse [ah-dress]
will you give me your address? est-ce que vous pouvez me donner votre adresse? [esker voo poovay mer doh-nay . . .]
adjust ajuster [ahjoos-tay]
admission *(to disco etc)* l'entrée [on-tray]
advance: can we book in advance? est-ce qu'on peut réserver à l'avance? [eskon per rayzair-vay ah lah-vons]
advert une annonce [ah-nons]
afraid: I'm afraid I don't know je regrette, je ne sais pas [jer rer-gret . . .]
he's afraid of . . . il a peur de . . . [eel ah per der]
after après [ah-pray]
after you après vous
afternoon l'après-midi [ahpray-mee-dee]
in the afternoon l'après-midi
aftershave un aftershave
again de nouveau [noo-voh]
against contre [kontr]
age l'âge [ahj]
under age mineur [mee-nerr]
ages très longtemps [tray lon-ton]
agent un représentant [rerpray-son-ton]
ago: a week ago il y a une semaine [eelyah . . .]
it wasn't long ago il n'y a pas longtemps [eelnyah-pah . . .]
how long ago? il y a combien de temps? [konb-yan . . .]
agree: I agree je suis d'accord [jer swee dah-kor]
it doesn't agree with me ça ne me convient pas [san mer konv-yan pah]
air l'air
by air en avion [ann ahv-yon]
by air mail par avion
with air-conditioning climatisé [kleemah-tee-zay]
airport l'aéroport [ah-ayroh-por]
alarm: give the alarm donnez l'alarme
alarm clock un réveil [ray-vay]
alcohol l'alcool [al-kol]
is it alcoholic? est-ce que c'est alcoolisé? [. . . alkolee-zay]
alimentation *food*

alive vivant [vee-v̅o̅n̅]
is he still alive? est-ce qu'il vit encore?
all *(everything)* tout [too]
(everybody) tous (toutes) [toos, toot]
it's all right, I'm all right ça va [sah vah]
all right! d'accord! [dah-kor]
that's all c'est tout [say-too]
thank you, not at all merci, de rien [mairsee der ree-ya̅n̅]
all night toute la nuit, **all day** toute la journée
all I have/want tout ce que j'ai/je veux [toos-ker . . .]
allergic: I'm allergic to . . . je suis allergique à . . . [jer swee ahlair-jeek]
allowed: is it allowed? est-ce que c'est permis? [eskersay pair-mee]
allow me . . . permettez-moi . . .
allumez vos phares *headlights on*
almost presque [presk]
alone seul [serl]
did you come here alone? est-ce que vous êtes venu ici tout seul? [esker voo zait ver-noo . . .]
leave me alone! laissez-moi tranquille! [lay-say mwah tr̅o̅n̅-keel]
already déjà [day-jah]
also aussi [oh-see]
although bien que [bee-ya̅n̅ ker]
altogether ensemble [o̅n̅-s̅o̅n̅bl]
what does that make altogether? qu'est-ce que ça fait au total? [kesker sah fay oh toh-tal]
always toujours [too-joor]
a.m.: 10 a.m. dix heures du matin [. . . doo mah-ta̅n̅]
ambassador l'ambassadeur [o̅n̅bah-sah-derr]
ambulance l'ambulance [o̅n̅boo-l̅o̅n̅s]
get an ambulance! appelez une ambulance!
» *TRAVEL TIP: no central number; in an emergency ring 'Police Secours'*
America l'Amérique [ahmay-rik]
American américain [ahmay-ree-ka̅n̅]
among parmi [. . . mee]
amp ampère [o̅n̅-pair]
15 amp fuse un fusible de 15 ampères [foo-zeebl . . .]

anchor l'ancre [o͞nkr]
and et [ay]
angry fâché [fah-shay]
don't get angry ne vous fâchez pas [ner voo fah-shay pah]
ankle la cheville [sher-vee]
anniversary: it's our anniversary c'est notre anniversaire de mariage [ahnee-vair-sair der mahr-yahj]
annoy: he's annoying me il m'importune [a͞npor-toon]
it's very annoying c'est très ennuyeux [o͞n-nwee-yer]
anorak un anorak
another: can we have another room? est-ce qu'on peut avoir une autre chambre? [esko͞n per ah-vwahr oon-ohtr . . .]
another beer, please encore une bière, s'il vous plaît
answer une réponse [ray-po͞ns]
to answer répondre
there's no answer on ne répond pas
antifreeze l'antigel [o͞ntee-jel]
any: have you got any bread/water? est-ce que vous avez du pain/de l'eau? [. . . doo pa͞n, der loh]
have you got any rooms? est-ce que vous avez des chambres? [. . . day sho͞nbr]
we haven't got any money/tickets nous n'avons pas d'argent/de billets [. . . dahr-jo͞n, der bee-yay]
I haven't got any je n'en ai pas [jer no͞nn ay pah]
anybody: is anybody there? est-ce qu'il y a quelqu'un? [eskeel yah kel-ka͞n]
we don't know anybody here nous ne connaissons personne ici [. . . pair-son]
anything: have you got anything for . . . est-ce que vous avez quelque chose pour . . . [. . . kelker-shoz . . .]
I don't want anything je n'ai besoin de rien [. . . ree-ya͞n]
aperitif un apéritif
apology des excuses [ex-kooz]
please accept my apologies je vous prie de m'excuser [jer voo pree der mexkoo-zay]
appellation contrôlée *quality label: a guarantee that a wine comes from one particular area*

appendicitis l'appendicite [ahpān-dee-seet]
appetite: I've lost my appetite j'ai perdu l'appétit [. . . ahpay-tee]
apple une pomme
application form un formulaire d'inscription [formoo-lair dānskrips-yōn]
appointment un rendez-vous
can we make an appointment? est-ce que nous pouvons prendre rendez-vous? [esker noo poovōn prōndr rōnday-voo]
appuyer *push*
apricot un abricot [ahbree-koh]
April: in April en avril [ān nah-vreel]
aqualung un scaphandre autonome [skah-fōndr ohtoh-nohm]
area la région [rayj-yōn]
in the area dans les environs [. . . ōnvee-rōn]
arm le bras [brah]
around *see* **about**
arrange: will you arrange it? est-ce que vous pouvez vous en occuper? [esker voo poovay voo zānn-ohkoo-pay]
it's all arranged tout est réglé
arrest arrêter [ahray-tay]
arrêt *stop*
arrival l'arrivée
arrive arriver [ahree-vay]
we only arrived yesterday nous ne sommes arrivés qu'hier
art l'art [ahr]
art gallery un musée [moo-zay]
arthritis: he has arthritis il a de l'arthrite [. . . der lar-treet]
artificial artificiel [ahrtee-fees-yel]
artist un artiste [ahr-teest]
as: as big/quickly as possible aussi [ohsee] grand/rapidement que possible
as much/many as you can autant [oh-tōn] que vous pouvez
do as I do faites comme moi [fait kom mwah]
as you like comme vous voulez [kom voo voolay]
ascenseur *lift*
ashore à terre [ah tair]

ashtray un cendrier [so̅n̅dree-yay]
ask demander [dermo̅n̅-day]
I didn't ask for that ce n'est pas ce que j'ai demandé [ser nay pah ser ker jay . . .]
could you ask him to . . . est-ce que vous pouvez lui demander de . . . [esker voo poovay . . .]
asleep: he's (still) asleep il dort [dor] (encore)
asparagus des asperges [ass-pairj]
aspirin une aspirine [aspee-reen]
assistant *(shop)* un vendeur (une vendeuse) [vo̅n̅-derr, vo̅n̅derz]
asthma: she has asthma elle a de l'asthme [. . . der lassm]
at: at the cafe au [oh] café
at my hotel à mon hôtel [ah . . .]
at one o'clock à une heure
atmosphere l'atmosphère [atmoss-fair]
attractive: I think you are very attractive *(to woman)* je vous trouve très jolie [. . . joh-lee]
it's an attractive offer c'est une offre avantageuse [. . . ahvo̅n̅-tah-jerz]
aubergine une aubergine [ohbair-jeen]
August: in August en août [o̅n̅n-oot]
aunt: my aunt ma tante [to̅n̅t]
Australia l'Australie [ostrah-lee]
Australian australien [ohstrahl-ya̅n̅]
authorities les autorités [ohtoh-ree-tay]
automatic automatique
autumn: in the autumn en automne [o̅n̅n-ohton]
away: is it far away from here? est-ce que c'est loin d'ici? [esker-say lwa̅n̅ dee-see]
go away! allez-vous en! [ahlay voo zo̅n̅]
awful affreux [ah-frer]
axle l'essieu [ayss-yer]
baby un bébé
we'd like a baby-sitter nous cherchons quelqu'un pour garder les enfants [noo shair-sho̅n̅ kel-ka̅n̅ poor gahr-day layz o̅n̅-fo̅n̅]
back *(part of body)* le dos [doh]
I've got a bad back je souffre des reins [jer soofr day ra̅n̅]
I'll be back soon je reviens dans un moment [jer rerv-ya̅n̅ . . .]

can I have my money back est-ce que vous pouvez me rendre mon argent?
[esker voo poovay mer rondr . . .]
come back! revenez! [rerver-nay]
is he back? est-ce qu'il est de retour? [. . . der rer-toor]
I go back tomorrow je rentre demain [jer rontr der-man]
at the back derrière [dair-yair]
bacon le bacon
bacon and eggs du bacon avec des oeufs sur le plat [. . . ahvek day zer soor ler plah]
bad mauvais [moh-vay]
not bad pas mal [pah mal]
too bad! tant pis! [ton pee]
bag un sac
(handbag) un sac à main [sak ah man]
baggage les bagages [bah-gahj]
baignade interdite *no bathing*
baker's une boulangerie [boolonj-ree]
balcony balcon [bal-kon]
ball *(football etc)* un ballon [bah-lon]
(tennis, golf) une balle [bahl]
ball-point pen un stylo à bille [steeloh ah bee]
banana une banane [bah-nan]
band *(musical)* un orchestre [or-kestr]
bandage: could you change the bandage? est-ce que vous pouvez changer le bandage? [esker voo poovay shonjay ler bon-dahj]
bank *(establishment)* une banque [bonk]
(of river) la rive [reev]
» *TRAVEL TIP: opening hours 9-12 and 2-4; closed Sat (large towns) or Mon; early closing (noon) before a bank holiday and if bank holiday falls on Thurs may be closed on Fri as well; transactions carried out at one desk and money collected at another: 'la caisse'*
bank holiday un jour férié [joor fair-yay]
see **public holidays**
bar un bar
a bar of chocolate une tablette de chocolat [tah-blet der shohkoh-lah]
barber's le coiffeur [kwah-ferr]
bargain: it's a real bargain c'est une bonne affaire [sayt oon bon ah-fair]

barmaid la serveuse [sair-verz]
barman le barman [bahr-man]
basket un panier [pan-yay]
bath un bain [ba̅n̅]; *(tub)* une baignoire [bay-nwahr]
  can I have a bath? est-ce que je peux prendre un bain? [esker jer per pro̅n̅dr in ba̅n̅]
  bath towel une serviette de bain [sairv-yet . . .]
bathing costume un maillot de bain [may-yoh . . .]
bathroom la salle de bain [sahl der ba̅n̅]
  we want a room with private bathroom nous voulons une chambre avec salle de bain [noo voo-l̅o̅n̅ oon sho̅n̅br . . .]
battery une pile [peel]
  (in car) la batterie [bat-ree]
be être [aitr]
  I am je suis [jer swee]
  you are vous êtes [voo zait]
  he/she is il/elle est [eelay, ellay]
  it's c'est [say]
  we are nous sommes [noo som]
  they are ils/elles sont [eel s̅o̅n̅]
  he's been ill il a été malade [eel ah ay-tay . . .]
  don't be late ne soyez pas en retard [ner swah-yay pah zan rer-tar]
  I am cold/hungry j'ai froid/faim [jay frwah, f̅a̅n̅]
beach une plage [plahj]
  on the beach à la plage
» *TRAVEL TIP: topless bathing on most beaches; pay attention to safety warnings: red flag – no swimming; orange flag – unsafe, but lifeguard in attendance; green flag – swimming safe*
beans des haricots [ahree-koh]
  French beans des haricots verts [. . . vair]
  baked beans *not available as such*
beautiful beau (belle) [boh, bel]
  that was a beautiful meal ce repas était délicieux [ser rerpah aytay daylees-yer]
because parce que [pahrser-ker]
  because of the weather à cause du temps [ah kohz . . .]
bed un lit [lee]
  I am going to bed at 10 je vais me coucher à dix heures [jer vay mer kooshay ah . . .]

you haven't made/changed my bed vous n'avez pas fait mon lit/changé les draps [voo nahvay pah fay mōn lee, shōn-jay lay drah]
bed and breakfast *(terms)* la chambre et le petit déjeuner [lah shōnbr ay ler pertee dayjer-nay]
» *TRAVEL TIP: used to be non-existent as such in France, where there are so many inexpensive hotels; ask the local 'syndicat d'initiative' about the possibility of 'chambres chez l'habitant'*
bedroom une chambre [shōnbr]
bee une abeille [ah-bay]
beef du boeuf [berf]
beer de la bière [bee-yair]
draught beer bière pression [. . . prays-yōn]
» *TRAVEL TIP: for the equivalent of a half-pint of draught lager ask for 'un demi pression'; the standard measure is 330 cl (½ pint = 270 cl); if you simply ask for 'une bière' you may be served bottled beer (more expensive)*
before avant [ah-vōn]
before I leave avant de partir
I haven't been here before c'est la première fois que je viens ici [say lah prerm-yair fwah ker jerv-yān ee-see]
begin commencer [kohmōn-say]
beginner: I'm a beginner je débute [jer day-boot]
behind derrière [dair-yair]
Belgian belge [belj]
Belgium la Belgique [bel-jeek]
believe croire [krwahr]
I don't believe you je ne vous crois [krwah] pas
bell une cloche [klosh]
(at door) la sonnette [soh-net]
belong: that belongs to me c'est à moi [sayt ah mwah]
who does this belong to? à qui est ceci? [ah kee]
below au-dessous (de . . .) [oh der-soo]
belt une ceinture [sān-toor]
bend *(in road)* un virage [vee-rahj]
berries des baies [bay]
berth *(on ship)* une couchette [koo-shet]
beside à côté de [ah koh-tay der]
best: the best . . . le meilleur . . . [may-yerr]
it's the best holiday I've ever had ce sont les meilleures vacances de ma vie

better meilleur [may-yerr]
haven't you got anything better? est-ce que vous n'avez rien de mieux? [. . . ree-yan̄ der myer]
are you feeling better? est-ce que vous vous sentez mieux? [esker voo voo son̄tay myer]
I'm feeling a lot better je me sens beaucoup mieux
between entre [on̄tr]
beyond plus loin que [ploo lwan̄ ker]
bicycle une bicyclette [bee-see . . .]
bière (à la) pression *draught beer*
big grand [gron̄]
a big one un grand
have you got a bigger one? est-ce que vous en avez un plus grand? [esker voo zon̄n ahvay an̄ ploo gron̄]
bikini un bikini
bill l'addition [ahdees-yon̄]
could I have the bill, please? vous me donnez l'addition, s'il vous plaît [voom doh-nay . . .]
billets *tickets*
bin *(dustbin)* une poubelle [poo-bel]
bindings *(ski)* les fixations [feexahs-yon̄]
bird un oiseau [wah-zoh]
birthday: it's my birthday c'est mon anniversaire [ahnee-vair-sair]
happy birthday! joyeux anniversaire! [jwah-yerz . . .]
bit: a bit of that cake un morceau [mor-soh] de ce gâteau
just a little bit un petit morceau
that's a bit too expensive/far c'est un peu trop cher/loin [an̄-per troh . . .]
bite: insect bites les piqûres d'insectes [pee-koor dan̄-sekt]
I've been bitten *(insects)* j'ai été piqué [jay ay-tay pee-kay]
I've been bitten by a dog j'ai été mordu par un chien [jay aytay mordoo par an̄ shee-yan̄]
bitter amer [ah-mair]
black noir [nwahr]
he's had a blackout il a eu une syncope [san̄-kop]
blanket une couverture [koovair-toor]
bleach de l'eau de javel [ohd jah-vel]
bleed saigner [sayn-yay]

he's bleeding il saigne [sayn]
bless you! *(after sneeze)* à vos souhaits! [ah voh sway]
blind aveugle [ah-vergl]
blind spot l'angle mort [longl-mor]
blister une ampoule [onpool]
blocked *(pipe etc)* bouché [boo-shay]
(road etc) barré [bah-ray]
blonde une blonde [blond]
blood le sang [son]
blood test une prise de sang [preez der son]
his blood group is . . . son groupe sanguin est . . . [son groop son-ghan ay]
I've got high blood pressure j'ai de la tension [jayd lah tons-yon]
he needs a blood transfusion il faut lui faire une transfusion [trons-fooz-yon] de sang
blouse un chemisier [shermeez-yay]
blue bleu [bler]
board: full board la pension complète [pons-yon kon-plet]
half board la demi-pension
boarding pass la carte d'embarquement [. . . donbar-ker-mon]
boat un bateau [bah-toh]
body le corps [kor]
bodywork la carrosserie [kahross-ree]
boil *(on skin)* un furoncle [foo-ronkl]
(verb) bouillir [boo-yeer]
it's boiling ça bout [sah boo]
do we have to boil the water? est-ce qu'il faut faire bouillir l'eau? [eskeel foh fair . . .]
boiled egg un oeuf à la coque [ann erf ah lah kok]
bone un os [oss]
(in fish) une arête [ah-ret]
bonnet *(of car)* le capot [kah-poh]
book *(noun)* un livre [leevr]
(verb) réserver [rayzair-vay]
book of stamps carnet de timbres [karnay der tanbr]
can I book a seat? est-ce que je peux réserver une place?
we have booked a table for 2 nous avons réservé une table pour deux [noo zahvon rayzair-vay oon tahbl poor der]

booking office le guichet [ghee-shay]
bookshop une librairie [leebray-ree]
boot *(of car)* le coffre [kofr]
(shoe) une chaussure [shoh-soor]
booze: I had too much booze last night j'ai trop bu hier soir [jay troh boo . . .]
border la frontière [frōnt-yair]
bored: I'm bored je m'ennuie [jer mōn-nwee]
boring ennuyeux [ōn-nwee-yer]
born: I was born in je suis né en [jer swee nay ōn]
borrow: can I borrow . . .? est-ce que je peux emprunter . . .? [esker jer per ōnprān-tay]
boss le chef [shef]
both les deux [lay der]
I'll take both of them je prends les deux
bottle une bouteille [boo-tey]
(for baby) un biberon [beeb-rōn]
bottle-opener un ouvre-bouteille [oovr-boo-tey]
bottom: at the bottom of the hill au pied de la colline [oh pyay der lah koh-leen]
bowels les intestins [āntes-tān]
bowl une coupe [koop]
bowls *(game)* les boules [bool]
box une boîte [bwaht]; *(in theatre)* une loge [lohj]
boy un garçon [gar-sōn]
boyfriend: my boyfriend mon ami [ah-mee]
bra un soutien-gorge [soot-yān-gorj]
bracelet un bracelet [brahs-lay]
braces les bretelles [brer-tel]
brake *(verb)* freiner [fray-nay]
can you check the brakes? est-ce que vous pouvez vérifier les freins? [. . . lay-frān]
I had to brake suddenly j'ai dû freiner tout à coup [jay doo fray-nay too tah koo]
he didn't brake il n'a pas freiné
brandy le cognac [kohn-yak]
bread du pain [pān]
a loaf of bread un pain
sliced bread du pain en tranches [trōnsh]
wholemeal bread du pain entier [ōnt-yay]
could we have some bread and butter? est-ce que vous pouvez nous apporter du pain avec du beurre? [. . . doo pān ahvek doo berr]

» *TRAVEL TIP: French bread is an entirely new experience after the sliced loaf; ask for 'une baguette'* [oon bah-ghet] *(best eaten the same day)*

break casser [kah-say]

I think I've broken my leg/arm je crois que je me suis cassé la jambe/le bras [. . . jer mer swee kahsay lah jonb, ler brah]

the car broke down la voiture est tombée en panne [lah vwahtoor ay tōn-bay ōn pan]

breakable fragile [frah-jeel]

breakdown *(of car)* une panne [pan]

(nervous) une dépression nerveuse [daypress-yōn nair-verz]

breakfast le petit déjeuner [pertee dayjer-nay]

English breakfast un petit déjeuner à l'anglaise [. . . ah lōnglayz]

» *TRAVEL TIP: the French don't have a cooked breakfast; usually coffee with bread and butter or croissants; if you insist on an English breakfast, be prepared to pay more*

breast le sein [sān]

breath: he's getting very short of breath il a de la peine à respirer [eelah der lah pen ah respee-ray]

breathe respirer [respee-ray]

I can't breathe j'ai de la peine à respirer

bridge un pont [pōn]

(game) le bridge

briefcase une serviette [sairv-yet]

brighten up: will it brighten up later? est-ce que ça va s'éclaircir plus tard? [. . . sayklair-seer . . .]

brilliant brillant [bree-yōn]

bring apporter [ahpor-tay]

bring the case to my hotel apportez la valise à mon hôtel

Britain la Grande-Bretagne [grōnd-brer-tan]

British britannique [breetah-neek]

Brittany la Bretagne [brer-tan]

brochure un prospectus [prospek-toos]

have you got any brochures about . . .? est-ce que vous avez des prospectus sur . . .?

broken: it's broken c'est cassé [say kah-say]

my room/car has been broken into quelqu'un s'est introduit [say tān-troh-dwee] dans ma chambre/voiture

brooch une broche [brosh]
brother: my brother mon frère [frair]
brown brun (brune) [br$\overline{an}$, broon]
brown paper du papier d'emballage [pahp-yay d$\overline{on}$bah-lahj]
browse: can I just browse around? est-ce que je peux regarder? [esker jer per rergahr-day]
bruise une contusion [k$\overline{on}$tooz-y$\overline{on}$]
brunette une brune [broon]
brush une brosse [bross]
(painter's) un pinceau [p$\overline{an}$-soh]
Brussels sprouts des choux de Bruxelles [shoo der broo-sel]
bucket un seau [soh]
buffet un buffet [boo-fay]
buffet car un wagon restaurant [vah-g$\overline{on}$ . . .]
building un bâtiment [bahtee-m$\overline{on}$]
(residential) un immeuble [ee-merbl]
bulb une ampoule [$\overline{on}$-pool]
the bulb's gone l'ampoule a sauté [l$\overline{on}$-pool ah sohtay]
a 100 watt bulb une ampoule de cent watts [. . . der s$\overline{on}$ wat]
bump: he's had a bump on the head il s'est tapé la tête [eel say tah-pay lah tet]
bumper le pare-chocs [par-shock]
bunch of flowers un bouquet [boo-kay]
bunk une couchette [koo-shet]
bunk beds des lits superposés [lee soopair-poh-zay]
buoy une bouée [boo-ay]
burglar un cambrioleur [k$\overline{on}$bree-oh-lerr]
our flat's been burgled on a cambriolé [k$\overline{on}$bree-oh-lay] notre appartement
burn: can you give me something for burns? est-ce que vous avez quelque chose pour les brûlures? [esker voo zah-vay kelker-shohz poor lay broo-loor]
this meat is burnt cette viande est brûlée [broo-lay]
my arms are burnt j'ai un coup de soleil aux bras [jay $\overline{an}$ koo der soh-lay . . .]
bus l'autobus [otoh-booss]
by bus en autobus
bus stop l'arrêt d'autobus [ahray . . .]
bus station la gare routière [gahr root-yair]

could you tell me when we get there? est-ce que vous pouvez m'avertir quand on y arrive? [esker voo poovay mahvair-teer kān tōn nee ah-reev]
» *TRAVEL TIP: pay-as-you-enter in most cities; you can buy a 'carnet de tickets' (book of tickets) from a newsagent; you must punch your ticket when boarding the bus and use 2 tickets if you are travelling further than two fare stages as shown on the bus route chart; runabout 'billets touristiques' available for bus and underground services*
business les affaires [ah-fair]
(firm) une entreprise [ōntrer-preez]
I'm here on business je suis ici pour affaires [jer swee zeesee . . .]
business trip un voyage [voh-yahj] d'affaires
it's none of your business cela ne vous regarde pas [ser-lah ner voo rer-gard pah]
bust la poitrine [pwah-treen]
» *TRAVEL TIP: bust measurements*

UK	*32*	*34*	*36*	*38*	*40*
France	*80*	*87*	*91*	*97*	*102*

busy occupé [ohkoo-pay]
are you busy? est-ce que vous êtes occupé?
but mais [may]
butcher's une boucherie [boosh-ree]
butter du beurre [berr]
button un bouton [boo-tōn]
buy acheter [ash-tay]
I'll buy it je l'achète [jer lah-shet]
by: I'm here by myself je suis venu seul [jer swee vernoo serl]
are you here by yourself? est-ce que vous êtes venu seul?
can you do it by tomorrow? est-ce que vous pouvez le faire d'ici à demain? [. . . dee-see ah der-mān]
by train/car/plane en [ōn] train/voiture/avion
by the church près de l'église [pray der . . .]
who's it made by? c'est fabriqué par qui?
cabaret un spectacle [spek-tahkl] de variétés
cabbage un chou [shoo]
cabin *(on ship)* une cabine [kah-been]
cable un câble [kahbl]
cable car un téléphérique [taylay-fay-reek]

cafe un restaurant-snack
» *TRAVEL TIP: the equivalent of a transport cafe is called 'relais routier', where good and relatively inexpensive meals can be had*
café *the usual place for a drink; waiter service, children usually welcome; drinks cheaper at the bar; snacks or set lunch usually available; you can telephone from a 'café' and there is often a special counter where stamps and tobacco are sold: look for a red diamond shaped 'TABAC' sign outside; you generally pay for your drinks on leaving*
cake un gâteau [gah-toh]
(small) un petit gâteau
caisse *cash desk*
calculator un calculateur [kalkoo-lah-terr]
call: will you call the manager est-ce que vous pouvez appeler le gérant [. . . ap-lay ler jay-ro̅n̅]
what is this called? comment ça s'appelle? [komo̅n̅ sah sah-pel]
call box une cabine téléphonique [kah-been taylay-foh-neek]
see also **telephone**
calm calme
calm down! calmez-vous! [kalmay-voo]
camera un appareil-photo [appah-rey . . .]
camp: where can we camp? où est-ce qu'on peut camper? [wesko̅n̅ per ko̅n̅-pay]
can we camp here? est-ce qu'on peut camper ici?
we are on a camping holiday nous faisons [fer-zo̅n̅] du camping
campsite un terrain [tay-ra̅n̅] de camping
» *TRAVEL TIP: enquire at the local 'syndicat d'initiative' (tourist office) about location, rates and facilities; you may have to leave your passport at the campsite reception desk; International Camping Carnet not essential, but it may help or entitle you to a discount*
can[1]: a can of beer une bière en boîte
(NB: *bottled beer is the rule*)
can-opener un ouvre-boîte [oovr-bwaht]
can[2]: can I have . . .? est-ce que je peux avoir . . .? [esker jer per ah-vwahr]
can you show me . . .? est-ce que vous pouvez me montrer . . .?

I can't swim je ne sais pas nager [jer ner say pah]
he can't... il ne peut pas...
we can't... nous ne pouvons [poo-vōn] pas...
Canada le Canada [kahnah-dah]
Canadian canadien [kahnahd-yān]
cancel: I want to cancel my booking je veux annuler ma réservation [jer ver ahnoo-lay mah rayzair-vahs-yōn]
can we cancel dinner for tonight? est-ce que nous pouvons décommander le dîner ce soir? [... day-koh-mōn day ler dee-nay...]
candle une bougie [boo-jee]
capsize chavirer [shahvee-ray]
car une voiture [vwah-toor]
car keys les clés de la voiture [klay...]
by car en voiture
car park un parking
carafe une carafe [kah-raf]
caravan une caravane [kahrah-van]
caravan site un camping pour caravanes
carburettor le carburateur [karboo-rah-terr]
card une carte
do you play cards? est-ce que vous jouez aux cartes? [esker voo jway oh kart]
care: will you take care of this for me? est-ce que vous pouvez vous en occuper? [... voo-zōn noh-koo-pay]
goodbye, take care au revoir [oh rer-vwahr]
careful: be careful soyez prudent [swah-yay-proo-dōn]
car-ferry un ferry
carnation un oeillet [er-yay]
carpet un tapis [tah-pee]
carrots des carottes [kah-rot]
carry porter [por-tay]
will you carry this for me? est-ce que vous pouvez me porter ça? [esker voo poovay mer pohr-tay sah]
carry-cot un porte-bébé [pohrt-baybay]
cartridge une cartouche [kahr-toosh]
carving une sculpture [skoolp-toor]
case *(suitcase)* une valise [vah-leez]
cash: I haven't any cash je n'ai pas d'argent liquide [jer nay pah dahr-jōn-lee-keed]

will you cash a cheque for me? est-ce que vous pouvez me payer [pay-yay] un chèque?
I'll pay cash je paye comptant [jer pay kōn-tōn]
cash desk la caisse [kes]
casino un casino [kahzee-no]
casse-croûte *snack(s)*
cassette une cassette [kah-set]
castle un château [shah-toh]
» *TRAVEL TIP: most castles and museums are closed on Tuesdays in France*
cat un chat [shah]
catch attraper [ahtrah-pay]
where do we catch the bus? où est-ce qu'on prend l'autobus? [weskōn-prōn-lohtoh-boos]
he's caught a bug il a attrapé un virus [vee-roos]
cathedral la cathédrale [kahtay-drahl]
catholic catholique [kahtoh-leek]
cauliflower un chou-fleur [shoo-flerr]
cave une grotte [grot]
ceiling le plafond [plah-fōn]
celery du céleri en branche [sail-ree ōn brōnsh]
» *TRAVEL TIP: if you see 'céleri' on the menu, it will probably be 'celeriac'; 'céleri rémoulade' is a celeriac salad eaten as a first course*
centigrade centigrade [sōntee-grad]
» *TRAVEL TIP: to convert C to F*

$$\frac{C}{5} \times 9 + 32 = F$$

centigrade	*−5*	*0*	*10*	*15*	*21*	*30*	*36,9*
Fahrenheit	*23*	*32*	*50*	*59*	*70*	*86*	*98.4*

centimetre un centimètre [sōntee-maitr]
» *TRAVEL TIP: 1 cm = 0.39 inches*
central central [sōn-trahl]
with central heating avec le chauffage [shoh-fahj] central
centre le centre [sōntr]
centre-ville *city centre, town centre*
cereal: *name the one you want:* 'les Corn Flakes' *is the best known*
certain certain (certaine) [sair-tān, –ten]
are you certain? est-ce que vous en êtes sûr? [esker voo zōn nait soor]
certificate un certificat [sairtee-fee-kah]

chain une chaîne [shairn]
chair une chaise [shairz]
(easy chair) un fauteuil [foh-ter]
chairlift un télésiège [taylays-yej]
chambermaid la femme de chambre [fam der shonbr]
chambres *rooms to let*
champagne du champagne [shon-pan]
change changer [shon-jay]
where can I change some money? où est-ce que je peux changer de l'argent? [wesker jer per shon-jay der lahr-jon]
could you change this into francs? est-ce que vous pouvez me changer ça en francs? [. . . mer shon-jay sah on fron]
I haven't any change je n'ai pas de monnaie [jer nay pah der moh-nay]
do you have change for 10 francs? est-ce que vous avez la monnaie de dix francs?
small change de la petite monnaie
do we have to change trains? est-ce qu'il faut changer? [eskeel foh . . .]
where can I get changed? où est-ce que je peux me changer?
» *TRAVEL TIP: changing money: remember you can buy up to £50 worth of foreign currency with your own cheques and a valid banker's card with Eurocheque symbol; exchange rate most favourable in a bank*
Channel: the Channel la Manche [monsh]
Channel Islands les îles anglo-normandes [eel on-gloh nor-mond]
chantier *roadworks*
charge: what will you charge? combien est-ce que ça va coûter? [konb-yan esker sah vah koo-tay]
who's in charge? qui est le responsable [responsahbl] ici?
chart *(map)* une carte maritime [. . . mahree-teem]
chaud *hot*
chaussée verglacée *icy road surface*
cheap bon marché [bon mahr-shay]
is there anything cheaper? est-ce qu'il y a quelque chose de meilleur marché? [. . . may-yer mahr-shay]
cheat: I've been cheated je me suis fait avoir [jer mer swee fay ah-vwahr]

check: will you check? est-ce que vous pouvez vérifier [. . . vayreef-yay]
I'm sure, I've checked j'en suis sûr, j'ai vérifié
we checked in/we checked out at 10 nous sommes arrivés/partis à dix heures
cheek *(part of face)* la joue [joo]
cheers! *(toast)* santé! [son-tay]
cheerio *(bye)* au revoir! [oh rer-vwahr]
cheese du fromage [froh-mahj]
mild/strong cheese du fromage doux/fort [. . . doo, for]
» *TRAVEL TIP: cheese is always served before the sweet course; don't ask for biscuits, as bread is usually eaten with cheese; there is a bewildering variety of cheeses: ask to sample before buying*
chef le chef cuisinier [. . . kweezeen-yay]
chemist's une pharmacie [farmah-see]
» *TRAVEL TIP: often with green cross sign; most will make up a prescription; address of chemist on all-night or Sunday duty ('pharmacie de garde') in local paper or on door of every 'pharmacie'*
cheque un chèque [shek]
cheque book le carnet de chèques
cheque card la carte d'identité bancaire [kart deedon-tee-tay bon-kair]
» *TRAVEL TIP: you won't be able to pay in a shop with your own cheques, but remember you can buy foreign currency with your cheques and your Eurocard*
chess les échecs [ay-sheck]
chest la poitrine [pwah-treen]
» *TRAVEL TIP: chest measurements ('tour de poitrine')*

UK	*34*	*36*	*38*	*40*	*42*	*44*	*46*
France	*87*	*91*	*97*	*102*	*107*	*112*	*117*

cherries des cerises [ser-reez]
chewing gum du chewing-gum [shween-gom]
chicken du poulet [poo-lay]
chickenpox la varicelle [vahree-sel]
child un enfant [on-fon]
my children mes enfants
children's portions des portions [pors-yon] pour enfants
» *TRAVEL TIP: children are generally welcome in restaurants and cafés*

chin le menton [mon-ton]
china la porcelaine [por-ser-lain]
chips des frites [freet]
(at casino) des plaques [plak]
chocolate du chocolat [shohkoh-lah]
a box of chocolates une boîte [bwaht] de chocolats
hot chocolate un chocolat chaud [. . . shoh]
milk chocolate du chocolat au lait [. . . oh-lay]
plain chocolate du chocolat à croquer [. . . ah kroh-kay]
choke *(car)* le starter [star-tair]
chop: a pork chop une côtelette de porc [koht-let der por]
Christian name le prénom [pray-non]
Christmas: at Christmas à Noël [noh-el]
on Christmas Eve la veille [vey] de Noël
Happy Christmas joyeux [jwah-yer] Noël
» *TRAVEL TIP: Christmas Eve is usually an occasion for a big meal with the family or friends, 'le réveillon'* [rayvay-yon]
church une église [ay-gleez]
» *TRAVEL TIP: France being largely a catholic country there are few protestant churches; ask for 'le temple'* [tonpl]; *in big cities, you may find 'une église anglicane'* [onglee-kan] *(C. of E.)*
chutes de pierres *falling rocks*
cider du cidre [seedr]
cigar un cigare [see-gar]
cigarette une cigarette [seegah-ret]
would you like a cigarette? est-ce que je peux vous offrir une cigarette?
[esker jer per voo zoh-freer . . .]
tipped filtre
plain sans filtre [son feeltr]
cine-camera une caméra [kahmay-rah]
cinema un cinéma [seenay-mah]
» *TRAVEL TIP: tip the usherette; no smoking*
circle un cercle [sairkl]
(at cinema) le balcon [bal-kon]
circuit touristique *scenic route*
city une ville [veel]
city centre le centre-ville
[sontrer-veel]

claim *(insurance)* une demande d'indemnité [der-ma̅n̅d da̅n̅dem-nee-tay]
claret du bordeaux rouge [bor-doh rooj]
clarify clarifier [klahreef-yay]
class: 1st class, 2nd class première classe, deuxième classe [prerm-yair klas, derz-yem . . .]
clean *(adjective)* propre [prohpr]
can I have some clean sheets? est-ce que je peux avoir des draps [drah] propres?
my room hasn't been cleaned today on n'a pas nettoyé ma chambre aujourd'hui
it's not clean ce n'est pas propre
cleansing cream crème démaquillante [daymah-kee-yo̅n̅t]
clear: I'm not clear about it je n'ai pas bien compris
is the road clear? est-ce que la route est dégagée? [. . . daygah-jay]
clever intelligent (intelligente) [a̅n̅tay-lee-jon]
climate le climat [klee-mah]
climb: we're going to climb . . . nous allons escalader . . . [eskah-lah-day]
climber un alpiniste [alpee-neest]
climbing boots des chaussures d'escalade [shoh-soor deskah-lad]
» *TRAVEL TIP: beware of rapidly changing weather conditions; let somebody know where you plan to go; ask the local C.A.F. (Club Alpin Français) for information; the C.A.F. have an excellent network of huts ('refuges' and 'chalets-refuges')*
cloakroom le vestiaire [vest-yair]
(WC) les toilettes [twah-let]
clock une horloge [or-lohj]
close[1]: it's close today il fait lourd aujourd'hui [eel fay loor . . .]
is it close? est-ce que c'est près d'ici? [esker say pray dee-see]
close[2] *(verb)* fermer [fair-may]
closed fermé
when do you close? quand est-ce que vous fermez?
cloth le tissu [tee-soo]
(for wiping) un chiffon [shee-fo̅n̅]
clothes les vêtements [vet-mo̅n̅]
cloud un nuage [noo-ahj]

clutch l'embrayage [o͞nbray-yahj]
  the clutch is slipping l'embrayage patine [. . . pah-teen]
coach un autocar [otoh-kar]
  coach tour une excursion en autocar [exkoors-yo͞n . . .]
coast la côte [koht]
  coastguard le garde-côte [gahrd-koht]
coat un manteau [mo͞n-toh]
cockroach un cafard [kah-far]
coffee un café [kah-fay]
  white coffee café au lait [. . . oh lay]
  black coffee café noir [. . . nwahr]
» *TRAVEL TIP: if you want a small black coffee, ask for 'un café petite tasse', for a large black coffee: 'un café grande tasse'; white coffee as you know it is not served; 'café au lait' is hot milk with hot black coffee; 'café crème' is black coffee with a drop of milk or cream*
coin une pièce de monnaie [pee-yes der moh-nay]
  the coin is stuck la pièce est coincée [. . . kwa͞n-say]
coke *(drink)* un coca-cola
cold froid [frwah]
  I'm cold j'ai froid
  I've got a cold j'ai un rhume [jay a͞n room]
collapse: he's collapsed il s'est effondré [ayfo͞n-dray]
collar le col [kol]
» *TRAVEL TIP: continental sizes*

Continental	*36*	*37*	*38*	*39*	*41*	*42*	*43*
UK (old)	*14*	*14½*	*15*	*15½*	*16*	*16½*	*17*

colleague un(une) collègue [koh-leg]
collect: I want to collect . . . je viens chercher . . . [. . . shair-shay]
collision une collision [kohleez-yo͞n]
colour la couleur [koo-lerr]
  have you any other colours? est-ce que vous avez d'autres couleurs?
comb un peigne [pen]
come venir [ver-neer]
  I come/we come from London je viens/nous venons de Londres [jer vee-ya͞n, noo ver-no͞n . . .]
  when is he coming? quand est-ce qu'il vient? [ko͞ntesk-eel vee-ya͞n]

we came here yesterday nous sommes arrivés [noo somz ahree-vay] ici hier
come with me venez [ver-nay] avec moi
has he come back yet? est-ce qu'il est rentré?
come on! allons!
comfortable: it's not very comfortable ce n'est pas très confortable [. . . ko̅n̅for-tahbl]
Common Market le Marché commun [marshay koh-ma̅n̅]
communication cord le signal d'alarme [seen-yal dah larm]
company une société [sohsyay-tay]
I like your company j'aime votre compagnie [jaym vohtr ko̅n̅pah-nee]
compartment *(train)* un compartiment [ko̅n̅par-tee-mo̅n̅]
compass une boussole [boo-sohl]
compensation: I demand compensation je veux être dédommagé [. . . daydoh-mah-jay]
complain: I want to complain about . . . je désire réclamer au sujet de . . . [rayklah-may oh soo-jay der]
have you got a complaints book? est-ce que vous avez un registre [rer-jeestr] des réclamations?
complet *no vacancies*
completely complètement [ko̅n̅plet-mo̅n̅]
complicated compliqué [ko̅n̅plee-kay]
compliment: my compliments to the chef mes compliments [ko̅n̅plee-mo̅n̅] au chef
composter: prière de composter votre billet *please punch your ticket here*
compulsory: is it compulsory? est-ce que c'est obligatoire? [. . . ohblee-gah-twahr]
concern: I'm concerned about . . . je suis inquiet au sujet de . . . [jer swee a̅n̅k-yay oh soo-jay der]
concert un concert
concierge *caretaker*
concussion une commotion cérébrale [kohmohs-yo̅n̅ sayray-brahl]
condition: it's not in very good condition ce n'est pas en très bon état [ser nay pah o̅n̅ tray bohn ay-tah]
what are your conditions? quelles sont vos conditions? [kel so̅n̅ voh ko̅n̅-dees-yo̅n̅]
confection *ready-to-wear*

conference une conférence [konfay-rons]
confirm confirmer [konfeer-may]
congés *holiday*
congratulations félicitations [faylee-see-tahs-yon]
conjunctivitis une conjonctivite [konjonk-tee-veet]
connection *(train etc)* la correspondance [kohres-pon-dons]
connoisseur un connaisseur [kohnay-ser]
conscious conscient [kons-yan]
consciousness: he's lost consciousness il a perdu connaissance [. . . kohnay-sans]
consigne *left luggage*
constipation la constipation [konstee-pah-syon]
consul le consul [kon-sool]
consulate le consulat [konsoo-lah]
contact: how can I contact . . .? comment est-ce que je peux contacter . . .? [kohmon esker jer per kontak-tay]
  contact lenses les verres [vair] de contact
contraceptive un contraceptif [kontrah sep-teef]
convenient pratique [prah-teek]
cook cuire [kweer]
  it's not cooked ce n'est pas cuit [ser nay pah kwee]
  you are a good cook vous faites une excellente cuisine [voo fair oon exay-lont kwee-zeen]
  are there any cooking facilities? est-ce qu'on peut y faire sa cuisine? [eskon per ee fair . . .]
  cooker la cuisinière [kweezee-nyair]
cool frais (fraîche) [fray, fresh]
corkscrew le tire-bouchon [teerboo-shon]
corn *(on foot)* un cor au pied [kohrohp-yay]
corner *(bend)* un virage [vee-rahj]
  can we have a corner table? est-ce qu'on peut avoir une table d'angle? [eskon per ah-vwahr oon tahbl dongl]
cornflakes des cornflakes
correct correct
cosmetics des produits de beauté [prohdwee der boh-tay]
cost: what does it cost? combien ça coûte? [konb-yan sah koot]
cot un lit d'enfant [lee don-fon]
cotton du coton [koh-ton]

cotton wool du coton hydrophile [. . . eedroh-feel]
couchette une couchette [koo-shet]
cough la toux [too]
cough drops des bonbons [bōnbōn] pour la toux
cough mixture un sirop [see-roh] pour la toux
could: could you please . . .? est-ce que vous pouvez . . .? [esker voo poo-vay]
could I have . . .? est-ce que je peux avoir . . .? [esker jer per ah-vwahr]
we couldn't . . . nous n'avons pas pu . . . [noo nah-vōn pah poo]
country un pays [payee]
in the country à la campagne [ah lah kōn-pan]
couple: a couple of . . . quelques . . . [kelk]
courier l'accompagnateur [ahkōn-pahn-yah-terr]
course: first course l'entrée [ōn-tray]
main course le plat principal [plah prānsee-pal]
meat course le plat de viande [. . . vee-yōnd]
of course naturellement [nahtoo-rel-mōn]
court: I'll take you to court je vais vous poursuivre en justice [. . . poorsweevr-ōn-joos-tees]
cousin: my cousin mon cousin [koo-zān]
cover *(verb)* couvrir [koo-vreer]
keep him well covered couvrez-le bien
cover charge le couvert [koo-vair]
cow une vache [vash]
crab un crabe [krahb]
craft shop une boutique d'artisanat [. . . artee-zah-nah]
crash: there's been a crash il y a eu une collision [eelyah oo oon kohleez-yōn]
crash helmet un casque [kahsk]
crazy: you're crazy vous êtes fou (folle)
cream de la crème [kraym]
creche une crèche [kraysh]
credit card une carte de crédit [. . . kray-dee]
crêperie *pancake shop*
crisps des chips [cheeps]
cross *(noun)* une croix [krwah]
(verb) traverser [trahvair-say]
crossroads un carrefour [kar-foor]
crowded: it's crowded il y a beaucoup de monde [eelyah bohkoo-der-mōnd]
cruise une croisière [krwahz-yair]

crutch une béquille [bay-kee]
(crotch) l'entre-jambes [ōntr-jōnb]
cry: don't cry ne pleurez pas [pler-ray . . .]
cufflink un bouton de manchette [boo-tōn der mōn-shet]
cup une tasse [tahs]
a cup of coffee/tea un café/thé [kah-fay, tay]
cupboard une armoire [arm-wahr]
curry un plat au curry [plah oh ker-ree]
curtains les rideaux [ree-doh]
cushion un coussin [koo-sān]
Customs la douane [dwahn]
cut couper [koo-pay]
I've cut myself je me suis coupé [jer mer swee koo-pay]
cycle: can we cycle there? est-ce qu'on peut y aller à bicyclette? [eskōn per ee ah-lay ah beesee-klet]
cyclist un cycliste [see-kleest]
cylinder un cylindre [see-lāndr]
cylinder head gasket un joint de culasse [jwān der koo-lass]
damage: I'll pay for the damage je rembourserai les dégâts [jer rōnboor-ser-ray lay day-gah]
it's damaged c'est abîmé [. . . ahbee-may]
damp humide [oo-mid]
dames *ladies' toilets*
dance: is there a dance on? est-ce qu'il y a une soirée dansante? [eskeelyah oon swah-ray dōn-sōnt]
would you like to dance? voulez-vous danser? [voolay-voo dōn-say]
dangerous dangereux [dōnj-rer]
dark *(colour)* foncé [fōn-say]
dark blue bleu foncé [bler . . .]
when does it get dark? quand est-ce que la nuit tombe? [kōntesker lah nwee-tōnb]
darling: my darling *(to man)* mon chéri [mōn shay-ree]
(to lady) ma chérie [mah . . .]
dashboard le tableau de bord [tahbloh der bor]
date *(fruit)* une datte [dat]
(time) la date [dat]
what's the date today? quelle est la date d'aujourd'hui? [kel ay lah dat dohjoor-dwee]

can we make a date? est-ce que nous pouvons fixer un rendez-vous? [esker noo poovon feexay an ronday-voo]
it's the 1st of February c'est le premier février [prerm-yay . . .]
on the 2nd of February le deux février *(NB: except for the 1st of the month, use* 'deux', 'trois' *etc and not* 'deuxième' *etc)*
in 1983 en dix-neuf cent quatre-vingt trois [deez-ner-son kah-trer-van trwah]
daughter: my daughter ma fille [fee]
day un jour [joor]
by day de jour
the day after le lendemain [londer-man]
the day before la veille [vay]
dazzle: his lights were dazzling me ses phares m'éblouissaient [. . . maybloo-ee-say]
dead mort [mor]
deaf sourd [soor]
deal un marché [mahr-shay]
it's a deal! d'accord! [dah-kor]
will you deal with it? est-ce que vous pouvez vous en charger? [esker voo poovay voo zon shar-jay]
dealer: the BL dealer le concessionnaire British Leyland [konsess-yoh-nair . . .]
dear cher [shair]; *see* **letter**
December: in December en décembre [day-sonbr]
deck le pont [pon]
deckchair une chaise longue [shayz long]
declare: I have nothing to declare je n'ai rien à déclarer [jer nay ree-yan nah dayklah-ray]
deep: is it deep? est-ce que c'est profond? [esker say proh-fon]
défense d'entrer *no entry*
de-icer le dégivreur [day-jee-vrer]
delay un retard [rer-tahr]
the flight was delayed le vol a eu du retard [ler vol ah oo doo . . .]
deliberately exprès [ex-pray]
delicate délicat [daylee-kah]
delicatessen une épicerie fine [ay-pees-ree-feen]
delicious délicieux [daylees-yer]
deliver livrer [lee-vray]

delivery *(of goods)* la livraison [leevray-zōn]
(of mail) la distribution [deestree-boos-yōn]
de luxe de luxe [der-looks]
democratic démocratique [daymoh-krah-teek]
demonstration une démonstration [. . . –trahs-yōn]
(political etc) une manifestation [. . . –tahs-yōn]
dent une bosse [boss]
you've dented my car vous avez endommagé ma carosserie [. . . ōndoh-mah-jay . . .]
dentist un dentiste [dōn-teest]
YOU MAY HEAR . . .
ouvrez! *open wide,* rincez! *you can rinse now*
dentures un dentier [dōnt-yay]
deny: I deny it ce n'est pas vrai [ser nay pah vray]
deodorant un déodorant [day-oh-doh-rōn]
dépannage *breakdown recovery service*
departure le départ [day-par]
depend: it depends (on) ça dépend [day-pōn] (de)
deposit *(down payment)* un acompte [ah-kōnt]
(security) une caution [kohs-yōn]
(on bottle etc) la consigne [kōn-seen]
do I have to pay a deposit? est-ce qu'il faut verser un acompte? [eskeel foh vair-say ān ah-kōnt]
depressed déprimé [daypree-may]
depth la profondeur [prohfōn-derr]
desperate: I'm desperate for a drink je meurs de soif [jer merr er swahf]
dessert un dessert [day-sair]
» *TRAVEL TIP: always served after cheese*
destination la destination [destee-nahs-yōn]
detergent un détergent [daytair-jōn]
detour un détour [day-toor]
devalued dévalué [dayvah-loo-ay]
develop: could you develop these? est-ce que vous pouvez me développer [dayv-loh-pay] ces films?
diabetic diabétique [dee-yah-bay-teek]
dial le cadran [kah-drōn]
dialling code l'indicatif [āndee-kah-teef]
dialling tone la tonalité [tohnah-lee-tay]
diamond un diamant [dee-yah-mōn]
diarrhoea: have you got something for diarrhoea? est-ce que vous avez quelque chose pour la diarrhée? [. . . kel-ker shohz poor lah dee-yah-ray]

diary un agenda [ahjo͞n-dah]
dictionary un dictionnaire [deeks-yoh-nair]
didn't *see* **not**
die mourir [moo-reer]
he's dying il est mourant [moo-ro͞n]
diesel *(fuel)* du gas-oil [gahz-wahl]
diet un régime [ray-jeem]
I'm on a diet je suis au régime [jer swee . . .]
different différent [deefay-ro͞n]
can I have a different room? est-ce que je peux avoir une autre chambre? [esker jer per ah-vwahr oon ohtr sho͞nbr]
difficult difficile [deefee-seel]
digestion la digestion [deejest-yo͞n]
dinghy *(rubber)* un canot pneumatique [kah-noh pnermah-teek]
(sailing) un dériveur [dayree-verr]
dining car la voiture-restaurant [vwah-toor . . .]
dining room la salle à manger [sahlah-mo͞n-jay]
dinner le dîner [dee-nay]
dinner jacket un smoking
dipped headlights: I was using dipped headlights je roulais en code [jer roo-lay o͞n kod]
direct: does it go direct? est-ce que c'est direct? [. . . dee-rekt]
directory *(telephone)* l'annuaire [ah-nwair] du téléphone
dirty sale [sahl]
disabled handicapé [o͞ndee-kah-pay]
disappear disparaître [deespah-raitr]
disappointing décevant [days-vo͞n]
disco une discothèque [–tek]
discount un rabais [rah-bay]
disgusting dégoûtant [daygoo-to͞n]
dish un plat [plah]
dishonest malhonnête [mahloh-net]
disinfectant un désinfectant [dayza͞n-fek-to͞n]
dispensing chemist une pharmacie [fahrmah-see]
» *TRAVEL TIP: most 'pharmacies' are dispensing chemists*
distance la distance [dees-to͞ns]
in the distance au loin [lwa͞n]
distilled water de l'eau distillée [oh deestee-lay]

distress signal un signal de détresse [seen-yal der day-tres]

distributor *(on car)* le delco [del-koh]

district le quartier [kart-yay]

disturb déranger [day-ron-jay]

the noise is disturbing us le bruit [brwee] nous dérange

diving board le plongeoir [plon-jwahr]

divorced: I'm divorced je suis divorcé [jer swee deevohr-say]

do faire [fair]

how do you do? comment allez-vous? [koh-mont ah-lay voo]

can I do this? est-ce que je peux faire ça? [esker jer per fair sah]

what are you doing tonight? qu'est-ce que vous faites ce soir? [kesker voo fayt ser swahr]

how do you do it? comment est-ce que vous faites? [koh-mont esker voo fayt]

what did you do? qu'est-ce que vous avez fait? [kesker vooz ah-vay fay]

will you do it for me? est-ce que vous pouvez le faire pour moi?

I've never done it before je n'ai jamais fait ça [. . . jah-may fay sah]

I was doing 60 kph je roulais à soixante [jer roo-lay ah swah-sont]

doctor un docteur [dok-terr]

I need a doctor j'ai besoin d'un docteur [jay ber-zwan . . .]

YOU MAY HEAR . . .

est-ce que vous avez déjà eu ça? *have you had this before?*

où est-ce que ça vous fait mal? *where does it hurt?*

est-ce que vous prenez des médicaments? *are you taking any drugs?*

prenez-en deux, trois fois par jour/aux heures des repas *take two, three times a day/at meal times*

document un document [dohkoo-mon]

dog un chien [shee-yan]

don't *see* **not**

don't! non! [non]

door la porte [pohrt]

dosage la dose [dohz]
douane *Customs*
double double [doobl]
double room une chambre pour deux [shōnbr poor der]
double whisky un double whisky
douche *shower*
Dover Douvres [doovr]
down en bas [ōn-bah]
downstairs au rez-de-chaussée [rayd-shoh-say]
get down! descendez! [day-sōn-day]
drain *(in street)* un égout [ay-goo]
(in bathroom) le tuyau d'écoulement [twee-yoh daykool-mōn]
drawing pin une punaise [poo-nayz]
dress une robe [rohb]
I'm not dressed je ne suis pas habillé [. . . pahz-ahbee-yay]
» *TRAVEL TIP: sizes*

UK	*10*	*12*	*14*	*16*	*18*	*20*
France	*38*	*40*	*42*	*44*	*46*	*48*

dressing gown la robe de chambre [. . . shōnbr]
dressing *(on wound)* un pansement [pōns-mōn]
(in salad etc) l'assaisonnement [ahsay-zon-mōn]
drink *(verb)* boire [bwahr]
something to drink quelque chose à boire
would you like a drink? désirez-vous [dayzee-ray voo] boire quelque chose?
I don't drink je ne bois pas d'alcool [jer ner bwah pah dal-kol]
is the water drinkable? est-ce que l'eau est potable? [esker loh ay poh-tahbl]
drive conduire [kōn-dweer]
I've been driving all day j'ai roulé [roo-lay] toute la journée
I was driving c'est moi qui conduisais [kōndwee-zay]
driver le conducteur [kōndook-terr]
(taxi) le chauffeur [shoh-ferr]
driving licence le permis [pair-mee] de conduire
» *TRAVEL TIP: driving in France pay attention to 'priorité': as a rule cars coming from the right have right of way unless you are in a 'passage protégé', when you have the right of way; always have your licence ready*

droguerie *hardware shop*
drown: he's drowning il se noie [eel ser nwah]
drug un médicament [maydee-kah-mo̅n̅]
(narcotic etc) la drogue [drog]
he is on drugs il prend [pro̅n̅] des médicaments
drunk ivre [eevr]
dry *(adjective)* sec (sèche) [sek, sesh]
(verb) sécher [say-shay]
dry-clean nettoyer à sec [naytwah-yay ah sek]
dry-cleaner's une teinturerie [ta̅n̅toor-ree]
due: when is the bus due? quand est-ce que le bus doit arriver? [ko̅n̅t esker ler boos dwaht ahree-vay]
during pendant [po̅n̅-do̅n̅]
dust la poussière [poos-yair]
duty-free hors taxe [ohr-tax]
duty-free shop une boutique hors taxe
dynamo la dynamo [deenah-moh]
each chaque [shahk]
can we have one each? est-ce que nous pouvons en avoir un chacun? [. . .o̅n̅ nah-vwahr a̅n̅ shah-ka̅n̅]
how much are they each? combien est-ce qu'ils sont la pièce? [ko̅n̅b-ya̅n̅ eskeel so̅n̅ lah pee-yes]
ear l'oreille [oh-ray]
I have earache j'ai des douleurs [doo-lerr] à l'oreille
early tôt [toh]
we want to leave a day earlier nous voulons partir un jour plus tôt [noo voo-lo̅n̅ pahr-teer a̅n̅ joor ploo toh]
earring une boucle d'oreille [bookl doh-ray]
east l'est [est]
easy facile [fah-seel]
Easter Pâques [pahk]
at Easter à Pâques
Easter Monday le lundi [la̅n̅-dee] de Pâques
eat manger [mo̅n̅-jay]
something to eat quelque chose [kel-ker shohz] à manger
eau potable *drinking water*
egg un oeuf [erf]
Eire la République d'Irlande [. . . eer-lo̅n̅d]
either: either this one or that one ou celui-ci ou celui-là [oo serlwee-see oo serlwee-lah]
I don't like either aucun des deux ne me plaît [oh-ka̅n̅ day der . . .]

either would do ou l'un ou l'autre fera l'affaire [oo lan oo lohtr . . .]
elastic élastique [aylass-teek]
an elastic band un élastique
elbow le coude [kood]
electric électrique [aylek-treek]
electric blanket une couverture chauffante [koovair-toor shoh-font]
electric fire un radiateur électrique [rahd-yah-ter aylek-trik]
electricity l'électricité [aylek-tree-see-tay]
» *TRAVEL TIP: 220v the rule but 110v also in use: do check; 2-pin plugs widely used, also 3-pin plug; get an adaptor before you go, or buy a 'prise électrique' in a local supermarket*
électro-ménager *electrical appliances*
elegant élégant [aylay-gon]
else: something else quelque chose d'autre [kelker-shoz dohtr]
somebody else quelqu'un d'autre [kelkan dohtr]
somewhere else ailleurs [ah-yerr]
who/what else? qui/quoi d'autre? [kee, kwah dohtr]
or else . . . sinon . . . [see-non]
embarrassing embarrassant [onbah-rah-son]
embarrassed gêné [jay-nay]
embassy l'ambassade [onbah-sad]
emergency une urgence [oor-jons]
help me please aidez-moi s'il vous plaît [ayday-mwah see voo play]
» *TRAVEL TIP: emergency numbers on all telephone dials; 'pompiers' fire brigade; 'Police Secours' police*
empty vide [veed]
enclose: I enclose with my letter . . . je joins à ma lettre . . . [jer jwan ah ma laitr]
end la fin [fan]
when does it end? quand est-ce que ça finit? [kon tesker sah fee-nee]
enfants *children*
engaged occupé [ohkoo-pay]
(to be married) fiancé [fee-on-say]
engine le moteur [moh-terr]
engine trouble des ennuis mécaniques [on-nwee maykah-neek]

England l'Angleterre [ongler-tair]
  English anglais [on-glay]
  Englishman un Anglais
  Englishwoman une Anglaise [on-glayz]
enjoy: I enjoyed it very much j'ai beaucoup aimé [jay boh-koo ay-may]
  I enjoyed the meal j'ai très bien mangé [jay trayb-yan mon-jay]
enlargement *(photo)* un agrandissement [ahgron-dees-mon]
enormous énorme [ay-norm]
enough assez [ah-say]
  that's not big enough ce n'est pas assez grand
  I don't have enough money je n'ai pas assez d'argent
  thank you, that's enough merci, ça suffit [soo-fee]
enquiries office le bureau des renseignements [booroh day ronsayn-mon]
entertainment *(shows etc)* les attractions [ahtraks-yon]
entrance l'entrée [on-tray]
entry l'entrée [on-tray]
  entry permit un laisser-passer [laysay-pah-say]
envelope une enveloppe [onv-lop]
equipment *(sport etc)* le matériel [mahtayr-yel]
error une erreur [ay-rer]
escalator un escalier roulant [eskahl-yay roo-lon]
especially spécialement [spays-yahl-mon]
essential essentiel [aysons-yel]
Europe l'Europe [er-rop]
  European européen [er-roh-pay-an]
evacuate évacuer [ayvah-kooay]
even même [maim]
evening le soir [swahr]
  in the evening le soir
  evening dress la robe de soirée [rob der swah-ray]
ever: have you ever been to . . .? est-ce que vous êtes déjà allé à . . .? [esker voo zait day-jah ahlay ah]
every chaque [shahk]
  every day chaque jour [shahk joor]
  everyone chacun [shah-kun], tous *(plural)* [toos]
  everything tout [too]
  everywhere partout [pahr-too]

evidence: to give evidence témoigner [taymwahn-yay]
exact exact [ayg-zakt]
example un exemple [ayg-zonpl]
  for example par exemple
excellent excellent [ayksay-lon]
except: except me à part moi [ah-par . . .]
excess *(insurance)* la franchise [fron-sheez]
  excess baggage un excédent de bagages [ayksay-don der bah-gahj]
exchange *(money)* le change [shonj]
  (telephone) le central [sontral]
  exchange rate le taux de change [toh der shonj]
excursion une excursion [exkoors-yon]
excuse me pardon Monsieur (*or* Madame, Mademoiselle) [pahr-don mers-yer, mah-dam, mahder-mwah-zel]
exhaust *(car)* le tuyau d'échappement [twee-oh dayshap-mon]
exhausted épuisé [aypwee-zay]
exhibition une exposition [expoh-zees-yon]
exhibitor un exposant [expoh-zon]
exit la sortie [sohr-tee]
expect: she's expecting elle attend un bébé [el ah-ton an bay-bay]
  I'm expected je suis attendu [jer swee ahton-doo]
expenses les dépenses [day-pons]
  it's on expenses ça va sur la note de frais [sah vah soor lah not der fray]
expensive cher [shair]
expert un spécialiste [spays-yah-leest]
explain expliquer [explee-kay]
export exporter [expohr-tay]
exposure: 24 exposure film un film de vingt-quatre poses [. . . pohz]
  exposure meter un posemètre [pohz-maitr]
express: I'd like to send it express j'aimerais l'envoyer par exprès [jaym-ray lonvwah-yay pahr ex-pres]
extra: is it extra? est-ce que c'est en supplément? [esker say on sooplay-mon]
  an extra blanket une couverture de plus [oon koovair-toor der ploos]

eye l'oeil [er-ee]
the eyes les yeux [yer]
eye bath une lotion [lohs-yo͞n] pour les yeux
eyeshadow le fard à paupières [fahr ah pohp-yair]
eye witness un témoin oculaire [tay-mwa͞n ohkoo-lair]
fabric un tissu [tee-soo]
face le visage [vee-zahj]
factory une fabrique [fah-brik]
Fahrenheit *see* **centigrade**
faint: she's fainted elle s'est évanouie [el sayt ayvah-nwee]
fair une foire [fwahr]
that's not fair ce n'est pas juste [ser nay pah joost]
faithfully *see* **letter**
fake faux (fausse) [foh, fohs]
fall tomber [to͞n-bay]
he's fallen il est tombé
false faux (fausse) [foh, fohs]
false teeth un dentier [do͞nt-yay]
family la famille [fah-mee]
do you have any family? est-ce que vous avez des enfants? [esker voo zah-vay day zo͞nfo͞n]
fan *(in car, room etc)* le ventilateur [vo͞ntee-lah-terr]
(supporter) un supporter [soopohr-tair]
fan belt la courroie de ventilateur [koo-rwah . . .]
far loin [lwa͞n]
is it far? est-ce que c'est loin? [esker say lwa͞n]
how far is it? c'est à quelle distance d'ici? [say ah kel dees-to͞ns dee-see]
fare *(travel)* le prix du billet [pree doo bee-yay]
half fare le demi-tarif [der-mee tah-reef]
full fare le plein tarif [pla͞n . . .]
farm une ferme [fairm]
farther plus loin [ploo lwa͞n]
fashion la mode [mod]
fashion shop une boutique de mode
fast *(adjective)* rapide [rah-peed]
don't speak so fast ne parlez pas si vite [ner pahr-lay pah see veet]
fat gros [groh]
(on meat) du gras [grah]

father: my father mon père [pair]
fathom une brasse *(1.83 m)*
fault un défaut [day-foh]
there's a fault c'est défectueux [dayfek-too-er]
it's not my fault ce n'est pas de ma faute [ser nay pahd mah foht]
favourite préféré [prayfay-ray]
February: in February en février [fayvree-ay]
fed-up: I'm fed-up j'en ai assez [jōn nay ah-say]
fee: what's the fee? combien ça coûte? [kōnb-yān sah koot]
feel: I feel cold/hot j'ai froid/chaud [jay frwah, shoh]
I don't feel well je ne me sens pas bien [jern mer sōn pah bee-yān]
I feel ill je me sens mal [jerm sōn mal]
I feel sick j'ai mal au coeur [jay mal oh kerr]
I feel like *(I want)* j'ai envie de [jay ōn-vee der]
felt-tip pen un stylo-feutre [steeloh-fertr]
femmes *women*
fermé *closed*
ferry le ferry-boat [fairee-boht]
festival un festival [festee-val]
fetch: will you come and fetch me? est-ce que vous pouvez venir me chercher? [esker voo poovay ver-neer mer shair-shay]
could you go and fetch . . .? est-ce que vous pouvez aller chercher . . .?
fever la fièvre [fee-yaivr]
I am feverish j'ai de la fièvre [jay . . .]
few: few people peu de gens [per der jōn]
a few days quelques jours [kel-ker joor]
only a few seulement quelques uns [serl-mōn kelker-zān]
fiancé: my fiancé mon fiancé [fee-yōn-say]
my fiancée ma fiancée
fiddle: it's a fiddle c'est malhonnête [maloh-nait]
field un champ [shōn]
fig une figue [fig]
fight: there's been a fight il y a eu une bagarre [eelyahoo oon bah-gahr]
figure *(digit)* un chiffre [sheefr]
I'm watching my figure je surveille ma ligne [jer soor-vay mah leen]

fill remplir [rōn-pleer]
fill her up faites le plein [fait ler plān]
do I have to fill in a form? est-ce que je dois remplir un formulaire?
[esker jer dwah rōn-pleerr ān fohrmoo-lair]
fillet un filet [fee-lay]
filling *(in tooth)* un plombage [plōn-bahj]
film un film
I would like a 35 mm film j'aimerais un film 24 × 36
[jaym-ray ān film vānt-kat trōnt-sees]
a colour/b & w film un film couleur/noir et blanc
[. . . koo-lerr, nwahr ay blōn]
a 20 exposure film un film de vingt poses
[. . . der vān pohz]
filter un filtre [feeltr]
I was in the filter lane j'étais dans la voie de sortie
[jay-tay dōn lah vwah der sohr-tee]
find trouver [troo-vay]
if you find it si vous le (la) trouvez [see voo ler troo-vay]
I've found a . . . j'ai trouvé un . . . [jay . . .]
fine: the weather is fine il fait beau temps [eel fay boh tōn]
a 50 francs fine une amende de cinquante francs [oon ah-mōnd der . . .]
OK, that's fine d'accord, ça va bien [dah-kor sah vah bee-yān]
finger le doigt [dwah]
fingernail un ongle [ōngl]
finish finir [fee-neer]
I haven't finished je n'ai pas fini [jer nay pah fee-nee]
fire un feu [fer]
(blaze: house on fire etc) un incendie [ānsōn-dee]
(heater) un radiateur [rahd-yah-terr]
fire! au feu! [oh fer]
can we light a fire here? est-ce qu'on peut faire du feu ici? [eskōn per fair doo fer ee-see]
call the fire brigade appelez les pompiers [ap-lay lay pōnp-yay]
» *TRAVEL TIP: the fire brigade number 'pompiers' is on all telephone dials*
it's not firing *(car)* il y a un défaut à l'allumage
[eelyah ān day-foh ah lahloo-mahj]

fire extinguisher un extincteur [ex-tañk-terr]
fireworks un feu d'artifice [fer dahrtee-fees]
firm une entreprise [oñtrer-preez]
first premier [prerm-yay]
I was first j'étais le premier
first aid les premiers secours [. . . ser-koor]
first aid kit une trousse [troos] de premiers secours
first name le prénom [pray-noñ]
fish du poisson [pwah-soñ]
fishmonger's une poissonnerie [pwahson-ree]
fishing la pêche [paish]
fishing rod une canne [kan] à pêche
» *TRAVEL TIP: if you want to go fishing you will need a special permit, 'le permis de pêche'; enquire at the 'syndicat d'initiative'*
fit *(healthy)* en bonne condition physique [oñ bonn koñdees-yoñ fee-zeek]
it doesn't fit me ça ne me va pas [sann mer vah pah]
fix: can you fix it? *(repair)* est-ce que vous pouvez le réparer? [esker voo poo-vay ler raypah-ray]
(arrange) est-ce que vous pouvez arranger ça? [. . . ahroñjay sah]
fizzy mousseux [moo-ser]
flag un drapeau [drah-poh]
flannel un gant de toilette [goñ der twah-let]
flash *(photo)* un flash
flashcube une ampoule de flash [oñ-pool . . .]
flat plat [plah]
(noun) un appartement [ahpahr-ter-moñ]
I've got a flat *(tyre)* j'ai un pneu à plat [jay añ pner . . .]
can you repair a flat? est-ce que vous pouvez réparer une crevaison? [esker voo poovay raypah-ray oon krervay-zoñ]
flavour la saveur [sah-verr]
fleas des puces [poos]
flies *(on trousers)* la braguette [brah-get]
flight un vol
flippers des palmes [pahlm]
float flotter
floor: on which floor? à quel étage? [ah kel ay-tahj]
the ground floor le rez-de-chaussée [rayd-shoh-say]

the top floor le dernier étage [dairn-yay . . .]
on the floor par terre [par tair]
flowers des fleurs [flerr]
flu la grippe [grip]
fly *(insect)* la mouche [moosh]
we flew here nous sommes venus en avion [noo som ver-noo onn ahv-yon]
foggy: it's foggy il y a du brouillard [eelyah doo broo-yahr]
fold plier [plee-yay]
follow suivre [sweevr]
food la nourriture [nooree-toor]
food store un magasin d'alimentation [mahgah-zan dahleemon-tahs-yon]
food poisoning une intoxication alimentaire [antohksee-kahs-yon ahlee-mon-tair]
foot le pied [pee-yay]
» *TRAVEL TIP: 1 foot = 30.1 cm = 0.3 m*
football le football
for pour
we've been here for a week nous sommes ici depuis une semaine [noo som zee-see der-pwee . . .]
forbidden interdit [antair-dee]
foreign étranger [aytron-jay]
foreigner un étranger
forest une forêt [foh-ray]
forget oublier [ooblee-yay]
I've forgotten . . . j'ai oublié . . . [jay . . .]
don't forget n'oubliez pas [nooblee-yay pah]
fork une fourchette [foor-shet]
form un formulaire [fohrmoo-lair]
formal officiel [ohfees-yel]
fortnight: for a fortnight pour deux semaines [. . . der ser-mayn]
fortunate: we were fortunate nous avons eu de la chance [noo zah-von oo der lah shons]
fortunately heureusement [er-rerz-mon]
forward en avant [on nah-von]
could you forward my mail? est-ce que vous pouvez faire suivre mon courrier? [. . . fair sweevr mon koor-yay]
here is a forwarding address voici l'adresse où envoyer le courrier [lah-dress oo onvwah-yay . . .]

foundation cream un fond de teint [fon der tan]
fountain une fontaine [fon-tain]
fracture une fracture [frak-toor]
fragile fragile [frah-jeel]
franc un franc [fron]
  Swiss francs des francs suisses [. . . sweess]
  Belgian francs des francs belges [. . . belj]
France la France [frons]
free libre [leebr]
freezer un congélateur [konjay-lah-terr]
French français [fron-say]
  Frenchman un Français
  Frenchwoman une Française [fron-sayz]
  I don't speak French je ne parle pas français [jer ner pahrl pah fron-say]
fresh frais (fraîche) [fray, fraish]
freshen up: I'd like to go and freshen up j'aimerais faire un peu de toilette [jaym-ray fair an per der twah-let]
Friday vendredi [vondrer-dee]
fridge un frigo [free-goh]
fried frit [free]
  fried egg un oeuf sur le plat [an nerf soor ler plah]
  nothing fried pas de fritures [pah der free-toor]
friend un ami [ah-mee]
friendly sympathique [sanpah-teek]
from de [der]
  where is it from? d'où est-ce que ça vient? [doo esker sah vee-yan]
front: in front (of) devant [der-von]
frost le gel [jel]
  frostbite des gelures [jer-loor]
frozen gelé [jer-lay]
  frozen food des aliments surgelés [ahlee-mon soorjer-lay]
fruit des fruits [frwee]
  fruit juice un jus de fruits [joo der frwee]
  fruit salad une macédoine de fruits [mahsay-dwahn]
fry frire [freer]
  frying pan une poêle [pwahl]
full plein [plan]
fumeurs: non-fumeurs *no smoking*

fun: it's fun c'est amusant [sayt ahmoo-zōn]
we had fun nous nous sommes bien amusés [noo noo som bee-yān ahmoo-zay]
funny drôle [drohl]
furniture les meubles [merbl]
further plus loin [ploo lwān]
fuse un fusible [foo-zeebl]
fuss: I don't want any fuss je ne veux pas d'histoires [jer ner ver pah dees-twahr]
future: in future à l'avenir [ah lahv-neer]
gale une tempête [tōn-pet]
gallon un gallon [gah-lōn]
» *TRAVEL TIP: 1 gallon = 4.55 litres*
gallstone un calcul biliaire [kal-kool beel-yair]
gambling: I like gambling j'aime le jeu [jaym ler jer]
game un jeu [jer]
gammon du jambon [jōn-bōn]
garage un garage [gah-rahj]
» *TRAVEL TIP: ask for 'un devis' (estimate), 'une facture détaillée' (itemized bill), 'la durée des réparations' (estimated time for repairs); avoid M-way garages whenever possible*
garden un jardin [jahr-dān]
garlic l'ail [*as 'eye'*]
gas le gaz [gahz]
(petrol) de l'essence [ay-sōns]
gas cylinder une bouteille de gaz [boo-tay . . .]
gasket un joint [jwān]
gauge une jauge [johj]
gear *(in car)* la vitesse [vee-tess]
(equipment) le matériel [mahtayr-yel]
in 1st gear en première vitesse [prerm-yair . . .]
gearbox trouble des ennuis avec la boîte de vitesses [dayz-ōn-nwee ah-vek lah bwaht der vee-tess]
gear lever le levier de vitesses [lerv-yay]
I can't get it into gear je n'arrive pas à mettre la vitesse [jer nah-reev pah ah maitr . . .]
gentleman: the gentleman here told me . . . ce monsieur m'a dit . . . [ser mers-yer mah dee]
gents les toilettes (pour messieurs) [lay twah-let poor mays-yer]
genuine véritable [vayree-tahbl]
German allemand [al-mōn]

Germany l'Allemagne [al-mann]
gesture un geste [jest]
» *TRAVEL TIP: the French use their hands more than the British do when they speak; be prepared to shake hands as often as required*
get: will you get me a . . .? est-ce que vous pouvez me chercher un . . .? [esker voo poovay mer shair-shay]
how do I get to . . .? comment est-ce qu'on peut aller à . . .? [koh-mon eskon per ah-lay ah]
we got here last night nous sommes arrivés hier soir [noo somz ahreevay . . .]
when can I get it back? quand est-ce que je peux le ravoir? [kontesker jer per ler rah-vwahr]
when do we get back? quand est-ce que nous rentrons? [. . . ron-tron]
get down descendre [day-sondr]
when do I get off? où est-ce que je dois descendre? [wesker jer dwah day-sondr]
I can't get in je ne peux pas entrer [jern per pah on-tray]
get out sortir [sohr-teer]
I get up at 7 je me lève à sept heures [jer mer laiv . . .]
gin du gin [djeen]
gin and tonic un gin and tonic
girl une fille [fee]
my girlfriend mon amie [ah-mee]
NB 'fille' also means 'daughter'; 'jeune fille' [jern . . .] *is used of unmarried girl*
gîtes ruraux *self-catering accommodation*
gîtes d'étape *dormitory accommodation (for ramblers etc)*
give donner [doh-nay]
will you give me . . .? est-ce que vous pouvez me donner . . .? [esker voo poovay mer doh-nay]
can you give me back . . .? est-ce que vous pouvez me rendre . . .? [. . . mer rondr]
glad: I'm glad (to . . .) je suis content (de . . .) [jer swee kon-ton . . .]
glass un verre [vair]
glass of water/of wine un verre d'eau/de vin [vairdoh, vairder-van]
glasses: my glasses mes lunettes [loo-net]
gloves des gants [gon]

glue de la colle [kol]
go aller [ah-lay]
he's/they are going there on Sunday il y va/ils y vont dimanche [eel ee vah, eel zee vōn]
where are you going? où allez-vous? [oo ah-lay voo]
I'm/we are going there tomorrow j'y vais/nous y allons demain [jee vay, noo zee ah-lōn . . .]
he's gone il est parti [eelay pahr-tee]
we went to Italy last year nous sommes allés en Italie l'année dernière [noo somz ah-lay . . .]
can I have a go? est-ce que je peux essayer? [esker jer per aysay-yay]
my car won't go ma voiture ne part pas [mah vwah-toor ner pahr pah]
when does the bus go? quand est-ce que le bus part? [kōnt esker ler boos pahr]
go down descendre [day-sōndr]; **go in** entrer [ōn-tray]; **go on** continuer [kōntee-nway]; **go out** sortir [sohr-teer]; **go up** monter [mōn-tay]
goal un but [boot]
goat une chèvre [shaivr]
goat's cheese du fromage de chèvre [froh-mahj . . .]
God Dieu [dee-yer]
goggles des lunettes protectrices [loo-net prohtek-trees]
gold: a gold chain une chaînette en or [shay-net ōnn ohr]
YOU MAY HEAR . . .
c'est plaqué-or *it's gold plated*
golf le golf [gohlf]
golf course un terrain [tay-rān] de golf
good bon [bōn]
good! très bien! [tray bee-yān]
be good! soyez sage! [swah-yay sahj]
good luck! bonne chance! [bonn shōns]
good morning, good afternoon bonjour (Monsieur *or* Madame *or* Mademoiselle) [bōn-joor mers-yer, mah-dam, mad-mwah-zel]
good evening bonsoir (Monsieur *or* Madame *or* Mademoiselle) [bōn-swahr . . .]
good night bonne nuit! [bonn nwee]
Good Friday le Vendredi saint [vōndrer-dee sān]

goodbye au revoir! [oh rer-vwahr]
gooseberries des groseilles à maquereau [groh-zay ah mak-roh]
gramme un gramme [gram]
» *TRAVEL TIP: 100 grammes = 3½ oz*
grand grand [grōn]
my grandfather mon grand-père [grōn-pair]
my grandmother ma grand-mère [grōn-mair]
my grandchildren mes petits-enfants
my grandson mon petit-fils [pertee-fees]
my granddaughter ma petite-fille [perteet-fee]
grape un raisin [ray-zān]
grapes du raisin
grapefruit un pamplemousse [pōnpler-moos]
grapefruit juice un jus [joo] de pamplemousse
grass l'herbe [airb]
grateful: I'm very grateful to you je vous suis très reconnaissant [jer voo swee tray rerkoh-nay-sōn]
gratuit *free*
gravy la sauce [sohs]
grease *(noun)* la graisse [grays]
(verb) graisser [gray-say]
greasy graisseux [gray-ser]
great grand [grōn]
great! parfait! [pahr-fay]
green vert [vair]
greengrocer's un marchand de fruits et légumes [mahr-shōn der frweez ay lay-goom]
green card la carte verte [kahrt vairt]
grey gris [gree]
grilled grillé [gree-yay]
grocer's une épicerie [aypees-ree]
ground: on the ground par terre [par tair]
on the ground floor au rez-de-chaussée [rayd-shoh-say]
group un groupe [groop]
our group leader notre chef [shef] de groupe
I'm with the English group je suis [jer swee] avec le groupe des Anglais
guarantee une garantie [gahrōn-tee]
guest un invité [ānvee-tay]
(in hotel) un client [klee-yōn]
guesthouse une pension [pōns-yōn]

guide un guide [gheed]
a guidebook in English un guide en anglais [. . . ān̄n ōn̄-glay]
guided tour une visite guidée [vee-zeet ghee-day]
guilty coupable [koo-pahbl]
guitar: do you play the guitar? est-ce que vous jouez de la guitare? [esker voo jway der lah ghee-tahr]
gums les gencives [jōn̄-seev]
gun un revolver [rayvol-vair]
(rifle) un fusil [foo-zee]
gynaecologist un gynécologue [jeenay-koh-log]
hair les cheveux [sher-ver]
hairbrush une brosse à cheveux [bross . . .]
haircut une coupe de cheveux [koop . . .]
where can I get a haircut? où est-ce que je peux me faire couper les cheveux? [wesker jer per mer fair koo-pay lay sher-ver]
is there a (ladies') hairdresser's here? est-ce qu'il y a un coiffeur (pour dames) ici? [. . . kwah-ferr poor dahm]
hairdrier un sèche-cheveux [sesh sher-ver]
half la moitié [mwaht-yay]
a half portion une demi-portion [der-mee pohrs-yōn̄]
half an hour une demi-heure [der-mee err]
ham du jambon [jōn̄-bōn̄]
hamburger un hamburger [ōn̄berr-gherr]
hammer un marteau [mahr-toh]
hand la main [mān̄]
handbag un sac à main
handbrake le frein à main [frān̄ . . .]
handkerchief un mouchoir [moo-shwahr]
handle la poignée [pwahn-yay]
hand luggage les bagages à main [bah-gahj ah mān̄]
handmade fait à la main [fay ah lah mān̄]
handsome beau (belle) [boh, bel]
hanger un cintre [sān̄tr]
hangover la gueule de bois [gerl der bwah]
happen: what happened? qu'est-ce qui s'est passé? [keskee say pah-say]
I don't know how it happened je ne sais pas comment c'est arrivé [. . . koh-mōn̄ sayt ahree-vay]
what's happening? qu'est-ce qui se passe? [keskee ser pass]

happy heureux [er-rer]
harbour le port [pohr]
hard dur [door]
hard-boiled egg un oeuf dur [erf door]
push hard poussez fort [. . . fohr]
harm: can it do (him) any harm? est-ce que ça peut (lui) faire du mal? [esker sah per lwee fair doo mal]
hat un chapeau [shah-poh]
hate: I hate . . . je déteste . . . [day-test]
have avoir [ah-vwahr]
I have j'ai [jay]
he/she has il/elle a [eel, el ah]
we have nous avons [nooz ah-von̄]
they have ils/elles ont [eelz on̄, elz on̄]
do you have any cigars/a map? est-ce que vous avez des cigares/une carte? [esker vooz ah-vay . . .]
can I have some water? est-ce que je peux avoir de l'eau? [esker jer per ah-vwahr . . .]
I have to leave tomorrow je dois partir demain [jer dwah . . .]
we have to . . . nous devons . . . [noo der-von̄]
hayfever le rhume des foins [room day fwan̄]
he il [eel]
head la tête [tait]
headache un mal de tête [mal der tait]
I have a (bad) headache j'ai (très) mal à la tête [jay tray mal . . .]
headlights les phares [fahr]
» *TRAVEL TIP: flashing headlights doesn't normally mean 'after you'!*
head waiter le maître d'hôtel [meitr doh-tel]
head wind un vent contraire [kon̄-trair]
health la santé [son̄-tay]
your health! à votre santé! [ah vohtr son̄-tay]
healthy en bonne santé [on̄ bon . . .]
hear entendre [on̄-ton̄dr]
I can't hear je n'entends pas [jer non̄-ton̄ pah]
hearing aid un appareil acoustique [ahpah-ray ahkoos-teek]
heart le coeur [kerr]
heart attack une crise cardiaque [kreez kard-yak]
heat la chaleur [shah-lerr]
heat stroke un coup de chaleur [koo der . . .]

heater un radiateur [rahd-yah-terr]
heating le chauffage [shoh-fahj]
central heating le chauffage central [shoh-fahj son-trahl]
heavy lourd [loor]
heel le talon [tah-lon]
can you put new heels on these? est-ce que vous pouvez me refaire les talons de ces chaussures? [. . . mer rer-fair lay tah-lon der say shoh-soor]
height la hauteur [oh-terr]
I'm 5 ft 6 je mesure un mètre soixante cinq [jer mer-zoor an maitr . . .]
hello bonjour [bon-joor]
help aider [ay-day]
can you help me? est-ce que vous pouvez m'aider? [esker voo poo-vay may-day]
can anybody help? est-ce que quelqu'un [kel-kan] peut m'aider (*or* nous aider)?
thanks for your help merci de votre aide [mair-see der vohtr aid]
help! au secours! [oh ser-koor]
her: I know her je la connais [. . . lah . . .]
give her . . . donnez-lui . . . [. . . lwee]
give it back to her rendez-le lui
it's her c'est elle [sayt el]
her bag *etc see* **his**
here ici [ee-see]
high haut [oh]
higher up plus haut [ploo oh]
high chair une chaise haute [shayz oht]
hill une colline [koh-leen]
(on road) une côte [koht]
him: I know him je le connais [. . . ler . . .]
give him . . . donnez-lui . . . [. . . lwee]
give it to him donnez-le lui
it's him c'est lui
hire *see* **rent**
his, her, its son [son], sa [sah], *(plural)* ses [say]
it's his (her) bag, it's his (hers) c'est son sac, c'est le sien [. . . ler see-yan]
it's his (her) car, it's (his) hers c'est sa voiture, c'est la sienne [. . . lah see-enn] *(in the plural* les siens, les siennes)

hit: he hit me il m'a frappé [. . . frah-pay]
the car hit him la voiture l'a heurté [. . . err-tay]
hitch-hike faire de l'auto-stop [fair der loh-toh-stop]
hitch-hiker un auto-stoppeur [oh-toh stoh-perr]
hold tenir [ter-neer]
hold this tenez ça [ter-nay . . .]
I'm holding it je le tiens [. . . tee-yan]
hole un trou [troo]
holiday les vacances [vah-kons]
I'm on holiday je suis en vacances [jer sweez on . . .]
Holland la Hollande [oh-lond]
in Holland en Hollande
home: at home chez moi [shay mwah]
(back in Britain) chez nous [shay noo]
I'm homesick j'ai le mal du pays [jay ler mal doo pay-yee]
we must go home nous devons rentrer
hommes *men*
honest honnête [oh-net]
honestly? vraiment? [vray-mon]
honey du miel [mee-yel]
honeymoon: our honeymoon notre lune de miel [nohtr loon der mee-yel]
hope: I hope that . . . j'espère que . . . [jes-pair ker]
I hope so/not j'espère que oui/non
horizon l'horizon [ohree-zon]
horn *(car)* l'avertisseur [ahvair-tee-serr]
I sounded my horn j'ai klaxonné [jay klaxoh-nay]
horrible horrible [oh-reebl]
hors d'oeuvre les hors d'oeuvre [ohr dervr]
horse un cheval [sher-val]
horse-racing les courses de chevaux [koors der sher-voh]
hose un tuyau (souple) [twee-yoh soopl]
hospital un hôpital [ohpee-tal]
will he have to go to hospital? est-ce qu'il faut l'hospitaliser? [. . . lospee-tah-lee-zay]
» *TRAVEL TIP: free of charge in France provided you belong to a national insurance scheme in Britain; some 'cliniques' (private hospitals) are 'conventionnées', i.e. covered by reciprocal health agreements; get the special form from the DHSS*

host l'hôte [oht]
hostess l'hôtesse [oh-tess]
hot chaud [shoh]
(spiced) fort [fohr]
hotel un hôtel [oh-tel]
» *TRAVEL TIP: price is per room unless specified otherwise; breakfast extra; nominal charge for children sharing the room; tariffs must be displayed inside the room; there are plenty of inexpensive (one- and two-star) hotels in most towns; you may be asked to leave your passport at reception when booking in*
hotplate une plaque chauffante [plak shoh-fon̄t]
hot-water bottle une bouillotte [boo-yot]
hour une heure [err]
house une maison [may-zon̄]
housewife une ménagère [maynah-jair]
how comment [koh-mon̄]
how are you?, how do you do? comment allez-vous? [koh-mon̄t ah-lay voo]
how many?, how much? combien [kon̄mb-yan̄]
how much is it? combien ça coûte? [kon̄b-yan̄ sah koot]
how many days? combien de jours?
how long does it take to . . .? combien de temps est-ce qu'il faut pour . . .? [kon̄b-yan̄ der ton̄ eskeel foh poor]
how long have you been here? vous êtes ici depuis combien de temps? [vooz ayt ee-see der-pwee kon̄b-yan̄ der ton̄]
how often do the buses go? il y a des bus tous les combien? [eelyah day boos too lay kon̄b-yan̄]
how high/long/wide/deep is . . .? quelle est la hauteur/longueur/largeur/profondeur de . . .? [kel ay lah oh-ter, lon̄-gher, lahr-jer, prohfon̄-der der]
hull la coque [kok]
humid humide [oo-meed]
humour: you need a sense of humour il faut avoir le sens de l'humour [eel foht ah-vwahr ler son̄s der loo-moor]
hundredweight *1 cwt = 50.8 kilos*
hungry: I'm hungry j'ai faim [jay fan̄]
I'm not hungry je n'ai pas faim [jer nay pah fan̄]
hurry: I'm in a hurry je suis pressé [jer swee pray-say]

please hurry! dépêchez-vous [daypay-shay-voo]
hurt blesser [blay-say]
I hurt myself je me suis fait mal [jer mer swee fay mal]
it hurts here ça fait mal ici [sah fay mal ee-see]
my leg/arm hurts j'ai mal à la jambe/au bras [jay mal ah . . .]
husband: my husband mon mari [mōn mah-ree]
I: I am je suis [jer swee]; **I have** j'ai [jay]
ice de la glace [glahs]
ice-cream une glace
ice-cream cone un cornet de glace [kor-nay . . .]
iced-coffee un café glacé [kah-fay glah-say]
with lots of ice avec beaucoup de glace [ah-vek boh-koo . . .]
ice-rink une patinoire [pahtee-nwahr]
identity papers les papiers d'identité [pahp-yay deedōn-tee-tay]
if si [see]
if we could si nous pouvions [see noo poov-yōn]
ignition l'allumage [ahloo-mahj]
ill malade [mah-lad]
I feel ill je ne me sens pas bien [jer ner mer sōn pah bee-yān]
illegal illégal [eelay-gal]
illegible illisible [eelee-zeebl]
illness une maladie [mahlah-dee]
imitation-leather du simili-cuir [seemee-lee kweer]
immediately tout de suite [toot sweet]
import importer [ānpohr-tay]
import duty les droits d'importation [drwah dānpohr-tahs-yōn]
important: it's very important c'est très important [say trayz ānpohr-tōn]
impossible impossible [ānpoh-seebl]
impressive remarquable [rermahr-kahbl]
improve: I want to improve my French je veux améliorer mon français [jer ver ahmail-yoh-ray mōn . . .]
in dans [dōn]; **in France** en France [ōn . . .]
in London à Londres [ah . . .]
in 1982 en 1982 [ōn . . .]
is he in? est-ce qu'il est là? [eskeelay lah]

inch un pouce [poos]
» *TRAVEL TIP: 1 inch = 2.54 cm*
include inclure [an̄-kloor]
does that include breakfast? est-ce que le petit-déjeuner est compris?
is it included? est-ce que c'est compris dans le prix?
is everything included? est-ce que c'est tout compris?
incompetent incompétent [an̄kon̄-pay ton̄]
inconsiderate: he was inconsiderate il a manqué d'égards [eel ah mon̄-kay day-gahr]
incontinent incontinent [an̄kon̄-tee-non̄]
incredible incroyable [an̄krwah-yahbl]
indecent indécent [an̄day-son̄]
independent indépendant [an̄day-pon̄-don̄]
India l'Inde [an̄d]
indicator le clignotant [kleen-yoh-ton̄]
indigestion une indigestion [an̄dee-jest-yon̄]
indoors à l'intérieur [ah lan̄tayr-yerr]
industry l'industrie [an̄doos-tree]
infection une infection [an̄feks-yon̄]
infectious contagieux [kon̄tahj-yer]
inflate gonfler [gon̄-flay]
inflation l'inflation [an̄flahs-yon̄]
informal simple [san̄pl]
(not official) non-officiel [nonoh-fees-yel]
information: could you give me some information about . . .? est-ce que vous pouvez me renseigner sur [. . . ron̄sayn-yay soor]
do you have any information in English about . . .? est-ce que vous avez des informations en anglais sur . . .? [. . . dayz an̄fohr-mahs-yon̄ on̄n on̄-glay soor]
information office bureau de renseignements [boo-roh der ron̄sayn-yer-mon̄]
inhabitants les habitants [ahbee-ton̄]
injection une piqûre [pee-koor]
injured: he's been injured il est blessé [eelay blay-say]
badly injured gravement blessé [grahv-mon̄ . . .]
injury une blessure [blay-soor]
innocent innocent [eenoh-son̄]
insect un insecte [an̄-sekt]

insect repellent une crème anti-insecte [krem o̅n̅-tee . . .]
inside à l'intérieur (de . . .) [ah la̅n̅tair-yer der]
insist: I insist on it j'y tiens absolument [jee tee-ya̅n̅ apsoh-loo-mo̅n̅]
I insist on . . . je veux absolument . . . [jer ver . . .]
insomnia: I suffer from insomnia je souffre d'insomnie [jer soofr da̅n̅som-nee]
instant coffee du café soluble [kah-fay soh-loobl]
instead à la place [ah lah plahs]
instead of au lieu de [oh lee-yer der]
insulating tape de la bande isolante [bo̅n̅d eezoh lo̅n̅t]
insulation l'isolation [eezoh-lahs-yo̅n̅]
insult: he insulted me il m'a insulté [eel mah a̅n̅sool-tay]
insurance une assurance [ahsoo-ro̅n̅s]
which is your insurance company? quelle est votre compagnie d'assurance? [. . . ko̅n̅pah-nee . . .]
I'm insured je suis assuré [jer sweez ahsoo-ray]
intelligent intelligent [a̅n̅tay-lee-jo̅n̅]
interdit *forbidden*
interdit aux piétons *no pedestrians*
interesting: it's very interesting c'est très intéressant [say trayz a̅n̅tay-ray-so̅n̅]
international international [a̅n̅tair-nahs-yoh-nal]
interpret: would you interpret for us? est-ce que vous pouvez nous servir d'interprète? [. . . noo sair-veer da̅n̅tair-pret]
into dans [do̅n̅]
introduce: can I introduce . . .? puis-je vous présenter . . .? [pweej voo prayzo̅n̅-tay]
invalid un invalide [a̅n̅vah-leed]
invalid chair un fauteuil roulant [foh-ter roo-lo̅n̅]
invitation une invitation [a̅n̅vee-tahs-yo̅n̅]
» *TRAVEL TIP: take a present such as flowers or a cake, but never a bottle of wine*
invite inviter [a̅n̅vee-tay]
can I invite you out? puis-je vous inviter à sortir avec moi? [pweej vooz a̅n̅vee-tay ah sohr-teer ah-vek mwah]
invoice une facture [fak-toor]
Ireland l'Irlande [eer-lo̅n̅d]
Irish irlandais [eerlo̅n̅-day]

iron *(clothes)* repasser [rerpah-say]
(noun) un fer à repasser [fair ah . . .]
ironmonger's une quincaillerie [kan̄-kie-ree]
island une île [eel]
it: put it here mettez le (la) ici
it is here il (elle) est ici
where is it? *(a place etc)* où est-ce que c'est? [wesker say]; *(a particular object)* où est-ce qu'il (qu'elle) est? [weskeel ay]
give it to me donnez-le (la) moi
it's him c'est lui [say . . .]
it's not working ça ne marche pas [sah . . .]
Italy l'Italie [eetah-lee]
Italian italien [eetahl-yan̄]
itch: it itches ça démange [sah day-mon̄j]
itemize: would you itemize it for me? est-ce que vous pouvez me faire une facture détaillée [. . . fak-toor daytah-yay]
its *see* **his**
jack un cric [kreek]
jacket une veste [vest]
jam de la confiture [kon̄fee-toor]
traffic jam un embouteillage [on̄boo-tay-yahj]
January: in January en janvier [jon̄v-yay]
jaw la mâchoire [mah-shwahr]
jealous jaloux [jah-loo]
jeans des jeans [djeenz]
jellyfish une méduse [may-dooz]
jetty la jetée [jer-tay]
jeweller's une bijouterie [beejoo-tree]
jewellery des bijoux [bee-joo]
job un travail [trah-vie]
join: would you like to join us? est-ce que vous voulez venir avec nous? [. . . ver-neer ahvek noo]
joke une plaisanterie [playzon̄-tree]
you must be joking vous plaisantez! [voo playzon̄-tay]
jours fériés *bank holidays*
jour de fermeture *closed on . . .*
journey un voyage [voh-yahj]
July: in July en juillet [joo-yay]
jumper un pull [pool]
junction un croisement [krwahz-mon̄]

June: in June en juin [jwān]
junk du bric à brac [breekah-brak]
just juste [joost]
he's left just now il vient de partir [eel vee-yān der . . .]
just there/a little juste là/un petit peu
not just now pas pour l'instant [pah poor lāns-tōn]
that's just right ça va très bien [sah vah tray bee-yān]
keen: I'm not keen ça ne me plaît pas beaucoup [sahn mer play pah boh-koo]
keep: can I keep it? est-ce que je peux le garder? [. . . gahr-day]
keep the change: gardez la monnaie [gahr-day lah moh-nay]
you didn't keep your promise vous n'avez pas tenu votre promesse [voo nah-vay pah ter-noo vohtr proh-mess]
it keeps on breaking ça se casse tout le temps [sahs kahs too ler tōn]
how long does it keep? combien de temps est-ce que ça se garde? [. . . sah ser gahrd]
kettle une bouilloire [boo-ee-wahr]
» *TRAVEL TIP: not a national institution in France; don't necessarily expect to find an electric kettle in a rented flat etc; people tend to boil water in a saucepan*
key une clé [klay]
the key to no 7 please la clé de la chambre sept, s'il vous plaît
YOU MAY THEN HEAR . . .
je vous réveille à quelle heure? *when would you like to be wakened?*
kidneys les reins [rān]
(food) des rognons [rohn-yōn]
kill tuer [too-ay]
kilo un kilo [kee-loh]
» *TRAVEL TIP: conversion: kilos ÷ 5 × 11 = pounds*

kilos	*1*	*1.5*	*2*	*3*	*5*	*10*	*20*
lbs	*2.2*	*3.3*	*4.4*	*6.6*	*11*	*22*	*44*

kilometre un kilomètre [keeloh-maitr]
» *TRAVEL TIP: conversion: km ÷ 8 × 5 = miles*

kilometres	*1*	*5*	*10*	*20*	*50*	*100*
miles	*0.62*	*3.11*	*6.2*	*12.4*	*31*	*62*

kind: that's very kind of you c'est très aimable de votre part [say trayz ay-mahbl der vohtr par]
he's very kind il est très gentil [eel ay tray jon̄-tee]
kiss embrasser [on̄brah-say]
give me a kiss embrasse-moi [on̄brahs mwah]
kitchen la cuisine [kwee-zeen]
knee le genou [jer-noo]
knife un couteau [koo-toh]
knitting needle une aiguille à tricoter [ay-gwee ah treekoh-tay]
knock: I knocked at the door j'ai frappé à la porte [frah-pay . . .]
there's a knocking noise from the engine il y a le moteur qui cogne [eelyah ler moh-terr kee kon]
he was knocked down by a car il a été renversé par une voiture [eel ah ay-tay ron̄vair-say par oon vwah-toor]
knot un noeud [ner]
know savoir [sah-vwahr]
I don't know je ne sais pas [jer ner say pah]
I didn't know je ne savais pas [. . . sah-vay pah]
we don't know nous ne savons pas [noo ner savon̄ . . .]
I don't know him je ne le connais pas [. . . koh-nay pah]
I don't know the area je ne connais pas la région
do you know where/how? est-ce que vous savez où/comment? [esker voo sah-vay oo, koh-mon̄]
label une étiquette [aytee-ket]
laces des lacets [lay-say]
lacquer de la lacque [lak]
lady: the lady here told me . . . cette dame m'a dit . . . [set dam mah dee]
the ladies' les toilettes (des dames) [twah-let day dam]
lager une bière [bee-yair]
» *TRAVEL TIP: if you ask for 'une bière' you will automatically be served 'une bière blonde', which is lager-type beer (although it may taste different from what you are used to)*
lake un lac
lamb *(meat)* de l'agneau [ahn-yoh]
lamp une lampe [lon̄p]

lampshade un abat-jour [ahbah-joor]
lamp-post un lampadaire [lonpah-dair]
land *(verb)* atterrir [ahtay-reer]
(noun) la terre [tair]
landscape le paysage [pay-ee-zahj]
lane une allée [ah-lay]
(on motorway etc) une voie [vwah]
the outside lane la voie de gauche [vwah der gohsh]
language une langue [long]
large grand [gron]
laryngitis une laryngite [lahran-jeet]
last dernier [dairn-yay]
last year/week l'année/la semaine dernière
last night hier soir [yair swahr]
(during the night) la nuit dernière [lah nwee dairn-yair]
at last! enfin! [onfan]
late tard [tahr]
sorry I'm late je m'excuse, je suis en retard [jer mex-kooz jer swee on rer-tahr]
later plus tard [ploo tahr]
see you later à tout à l'heure [ah toot ah ler]
at the latest au plus tard
laugh rire [reer]
launderette une laverie automatique [lahv-ree ohtoh-mah-teek]
lavabos *toilets*
lavatory les toilettes [twah-let]
lawyer un avocat [ahvoh-kah]
laxative un laxatif [laxah-teef]
lay-by une aire de stationnement [air der stahs-yohn-mon]
lazy paresseux [pahray-ser]
leader le chef [shef]
leaf une feuille [fer-ee]
leak une fuite [fweet]
there's a leak in my ceiling il y a une fuite au plafond [. . . oh plah-fon]
gas leak une fuite de gaz
the petrol tank leaks le réservoir fuit [. . . fwee]
learn: I want to learn . . . je veux apprendre . . . [jer ver ah-prondr]
lease *(verb)* louer [lway]; *(noun)* le bail [bie]

least: not in the least pas du tout [pah doo too]
at least au moins [oh mwa̅n̅]
the least le moins
leather du cuir [kweer]
leave *(go away)* partir [pahr-teer]
we're leaving tomorrow nous partons demain [pahr-to̅n̅ . . .]
when does the bus leave? quand est-ce que le bus part? [. . . pahr]
we left Paris yesterday nous avons quitté Paris hier [nooz ah-vo̅n̅ kee-tay . . .]
I left two shirts in my room j'ai laissé deux chemises dans ma chambre [jay lay-say . . .]
can I leave this here/with you? est-ce que je peux laisser ça ici/vous laisser ça? [esker jer per lay-say sah ee-see, voo lay-say sah]
left: on the left à gauche [ah gohsh]
I'm left-handed je suis gaucher [jer swee goh-shay]
left-luggage (office) la consigne [ko̅n̅-seen]
leg la jambe [jo̅n̅b]
legal: is it legal? est-ce que c'est légal? [. . . lay-gal]
lemon un citron [see-tro̅n̅]
lemonade de la limonade [leemoh-nad]
lend: will you lend me . . .? est-ce que vous pouvez me prêter . . .? [. . . pray-tay]
length la longueur [lo̅n̅-gherr]
lengthen rallonger [rahlo̅n̅-jay]
lens *(of camera)* l'objectif [l'objek-teef]
Lent le Carême [kah-raim]
less: less expensive/far (than) moins cher/loin (que) [mwa̅n̅ . . . ker]
less milk/money moins de lait/d'argent
lesson: French/skiing lessons des leçons de français/ski [ler-so̅n̅ . . .]
let *(flat etc)* louer [loo-ay]
let me help laissez-moi vous aider [lay-say mwah vooz ay-day]
let me/him go laissez-moi/le partir
will you let me off here? laissez-moi descendre ici [. . . day-so̅n̅dr ee-see]
let's go to allons à [ah-lo̅n̅ ah]
let's go allons-y [ahlo̅n̅z-ee]
letter une lettre

are there any letters for me? est-ce qu'il y a du courrier pour moi? [. . . doo koor-yay poor mwah]
letterbox une boîte aux lettres [bwaht oh laitr]
NB: start a letter with 'Monsieur' (or 'Madame', 'Mademoiselle') where you would have used 'Dear Sir' etc, and with 'Cher Monsieur' etc where you would have used 'Dear Mr Drew' etc. End the letter with 'Veuillez agréer, Monsieur, l'expression de mes sentiments distingués', or with 'Veuillez recevoir, cher Monsieur, l'expression de mes meilleurs sentiments' (less formal)

lettuce une salade [sah-lad]
level: the oil level le niveau d'huile [nee-voh dweel]
level-crossing un passage à niveau [pah-sahj ah nee-voh]
liable responsable [respo̅n̅-sahbl]
librairie *bookshop*
library une bibliothèque [beeblee-oh-tek]
libre *vacant; free*
libre-service *self-service*
licence un permis [pair-mee]
lid un couvercle [koo-vairkl]
lie un mensonge [mo̅n̅-so̅n̅j]
can he lie down for a bit? est-ce qu'il peut s'étendre un moment [eskeel per say-to̅n̅dr a̅n̅ momo̅n̅]
life la vie [vee]
life assurance une assurance-vie [ahsoo-ro̅n̅s-vee]
lifebelt la bouée de sauvetage [boo-ay der sohv-tahj]
lifeboat le canot de sauvetage [kah-noh . . .]
life-guard le surveillant de plage [soorvay-ya̅n̅ der plahj]
life-jacket le gilet de sauvetage [jee-lay . . .]
lift: do you want a lift? est-ce que je peux vous emmener quelque part? [. . . vooz o̅n̅m-nay kel-ker pahr]
could you give me a lift (to Paris)? est-ce que vous pouvez m'emmener (jusqu'à Paris)? [. . . joos-kah . . .]
the lift isn't working l'ascenseur ne marche pas [lahso̅n̅-serr ner marsh pah]
light *(not heavy)* léger [lay-jay]
(not dark) clair [klair]
the lights aren't working *(house)* la lumière ne s'allume pas [lah loom-yair ner sah-loom pah]

(car) les phares ne s'allument pas [lay fahr . . .]
have you got a light? est-ce que vous avez du feu? [esker vooz ah-vay doo fer]
can you put the light on/turn the light off? est-ce que vous pouvez allumer/éteindre [ay-t$\overline{an}$dr] la lumière?
when it gets light quand il fait jour [k$\overline{on}$t eel fay joor]
light bulb une ampoule [$\overline{on}$-pool]
light meter le posemètre [pohz-maitr]
lighter un briquet [bree-kay]
like *(the same as)* comme [kom]
would you like . . .? est-ce que vous voulez . . .? [esker voo voo-lay]
I'd like a coffee *etc* j'aimerais un café *etc* [jaym-ray . . .]
I'd like to go j'aimerais partir
I like it ça me plaît [sah mer play]
I like you vous me plaisez [voo mer play-zay]
I don't like it ça ne me plaît pas
he doesn't like it ça ne lui plaît pas [. . . lwee play pah]
what's it like? c'est comment? [say koh-m$\overline{on}$]
do it like this faites comme ça [fayt kom sah]
one like that un comme ça [$\overline{an}$ kom sah]
lime un citron vert [see-tr$\overline{on}$ vair]
line la ligne [leen]
lip la lèvre [laivr]
lipstick du rouge à lèvres [rooj ah laivr]
lip salve de la pommade [poh-mad] pour les lèvres
liqueur une liqueur [lee-kerr]
list une liste [leest]
price list le tarif [tah-reef]
listen écouter [aykoo-tay]
litre un litre [leetr]
» *TRAVEL TIP: 1 litre = 1¾ pints = 0.22 gals*

pints	*0.44*	*0.87*	*1.75*	*3.50*	*5.25*
litres	*0.25*	*0.5*	*1*	*2*	*3*

little *(small)* petit [per-tee]
a little un peu [$\overline{an}$ per]
a little ice un peu de glace
a little more un peu plus [. . . ploo]
live[1]**: I live in London/England** j'habite à Londres/en Angleterre [jah-beet ah l$\overline{on}$dr, $\overline{on}$n $\overline{on}$gler-tair]

where do you live? où est-ce que vous habitez? [wesker vooz ahbee-tay]
live² *(TV)* en direct [on dee-rekt]
(wire etc) sous tension [soo tons-yon]
liver le foie [fwah]
liver pate du pâté de foie
loaf un pain [pan]
lobster une langouste [lon-goost]
local: a local wine un vin de la région [. . . der lah rayj-yon]
a local restaurant un restaurant du coin [. . . doo kwan]
is it made locally? est-ce que c'est fait ici? [esker say fay ee-see]
location de voitures *car hire*
lock: the lock's broken la serrure est abîmée [lah say-roor ayt ahbee-may]
it's locked c'est fermé à clé [fair-may ah klay]
I've locked myself out/in je me suis enfermé dehors/dedans [jer mer swee onfair-may der-ohr, der-don]
locker un casier [kahz-yay] (qui ferme à clé)
London Londres [londr]
lonely: I feel lonely je me sens seul [jer mer son serl]
long long [lon]
will it take long? est-ce que ça va prendre longtemps? [. . . sah vah prondr lon-ton]
we'd like to stay longer nous aimerions rester plus longtemps [nooz aymer-yon res-tay ploo lon-ton]
that was long ago c'était il y a longtemps [say-tay eel-yah . . .]
loo: where's the loo? où sont les toilettes? [oo son lay twah-let]
look: he looks ill/tired il a l'air malade/fatigué [eel ah lair . . .]
it looks unsafe ça a l'air dangereux [sah ah lair . . .]
it looks nice c'est joli [say . . .]
look at that regardez ça [rergahr-day sah]
can I look? est-ce que je peux regarder?
I'm just looking je regarde [jer rer-gahrd]
I'm looking forward to . . . je me réjouis de . . . [jer mer ray-jwee der]
I'm looking for . . . je cherche . . . [jer shairsh]

look out! attention! [ahtons-yon]
loose *(undone)* défait [day-fay]
lorry un camion [kahm-yon]
lorry driver un chauffeur de camion [shoh-ferr . . .]
lose perdre [pairdr]
I've lost my . . . j'ai perdu mon (ma) . . . [jay pair-doo . . .]
I'm lost je me suis perdu [jer mer swee pair-doo]
lost property office le bureau des objets trouvés [boo-roh dayz ob-jay troo-vay]
lot: a lot (of) beaucoup (de) [boh-koo der]
not a lot pas beaucoup
a lot more expensive (than) beaucoup plus cher (que) [. . . ploo shair ker]
lotion une lotion [lohs-yon]
loud fort [fohr]
speak louder parlez plus fort [pahr-lay ploo fohr]
à louer *to let*
lounge le salon [sah-lon]
departure lounge la salle d'embarquement [sahl donbar-ker-mon]
love: I love you je vous aime [jer vooz aim]
he's in love (with) il est amoureux (de) [eel ayt ahmoo-rer]
I love this wine j'aime beaucoup ce vin [jaim boh-koo . . .]
lovely *(view etc)* très joli [tray joh-lee]
(dish etc) délicieux [daylees-yer]
we had a lovely holiday nous avons passé de merveilleuses vacances [nooz ah-von pah-say der mairvay-yerz vah-kons]
low bas [bah]
luck: good luck! bonne chance! [bon shons]
you're lucky vous avez de la chance [vooz ah-vay der lah shons]
that's lucky c'est de la chance
luggage les bagages [bah-gahj]
luggage rack le porte-bagages [port-bah-gahj]
lumbago un lumbago [lanbah-goh]
lump *(on body)* une grosseur [groh-serr]
(of sugar) un morceau [mohr-soh]

lunch le déjeuner [day-jer-nay]
YOU MAY SEE OR HEAR . . .
plat du jour [plah doo jour] *set menu*
» *TRAVEL TIP: the set menu is generally well worth trying; in Switzerland, 'déjeuner' is commonly used for 'breakfast'; use 'dîner' for lunch*
lungs les poumons [poo-mo͞n]
luxurious luxueux [looxoo-er]
luxury: a luxury hotel un hôtel de luxe [. . . der loox]
mad fou (folle) [foo, fol]
machine une machine [mah-sheen]
Madam Madame [mah-dam]
made-to-measure fait sur mesure [fay soor mer-zoor]
magazine un magazine [mahgah-zeen]
magnificent magnifique [mahnee-feek]
maiden name le nom de jeune fille [no͞n der jern fee]
mail: can you mail this for me? est-ce que vous pouvez me poster ça? [. . . mer pos-tay sah]
is there any mail for me? est-ce qu'il y a du courrier pour moi? [eskeel-yah doo koor-yay poor mwah]
main principal [pra͞nsee-pal]
the main roads les grandes routes [gro͞nd root]
make faire [fair]
will we make it in time? est-ce qu'on y arrivera à temps? [esko͞nn ee ahreev-rah ah to͞n]
who is it made by? c'est fabriqué par qui? [say fahbree-kay par kee]
make-up le maquillage [mahkee-yahj]
man un homme [om]
the man at the desk said . . . le monsieur au guichet m'a dit . . . [ler mers-yer . . .]
manager: I would like to see the manager j'aimerais parler au directeur [jem-ray par-lay oh deerek-terr]
manageress la directrice [deerek-trees]
manicure: can I have a manicure? est-ce qu'on peut me faire les mains? [esko͞n per mer fair lay ma͞n]
many beaucoup [boh-koo]
many places/people beaucoup d'endroits/de gens
map une carte [kart]
a local map une carte de la région [. . . der la rayj-yo͞n]
road map une carte routière [. . . root-yair]
a map of Paris un plan de Paris [a͞n plo͞n der pah-ree]

March: in March en mars [mahrs]
margarine de la margarine [mahrgah-reen]
marina un port de plaisance [pohr der play-zōns]
mark une marque [mahrk]
market un marché [mahr-shay]
when is market day? quand est-ce que c'est jour de marché? [kōnt esker say joor der mahr-shay]
marmalade de la confiture d'oranges [kōnfee-toor doh-rōnj]
married marié [mahr-yay]
marry: we were married in 1960 nous nous sommes mariés en 1960 [noo noo som mahr-yay ōn . . .]
will you marry me? voulez-vous m'épouser? [voolay-voo maypoo-zay]
marvellous merveilleux [mairvay-yer]
mascara du mascara
mashed potatoes de la purée de pommes de terre [poo-ray der pom der tair]
mass *(in church)* la messe [mess]
massage un massage [mah-sahj]
mast mât [mah]
mat un petit tapis [per-tee tah-pee]
match: a box of matches une boîte d'allumettes [bwaht dahloo-met]
football match un match de football
material *(cloth)* du tissu [tee-soo]
matter: it doesn't matter ça ne fait rien [sah ner fay ree-yān]
what's the matter? qu'est-ce qui ne va pas? [keskee ner vah pah]
mattress un matelas [mat-lah]
mature mûr [moor]
maximum le maximum [maxee-mom]
may: may I have/take . . . ? est-ce que je peux avoir/prendre . . .? [esker jer per ah-vwahr, prōndr]
may we . . .? est-ce que nous pouvons . . .? [esker noo poo-vōn]
May: in May en mai [may]
maybe peut-être [pert-aitr]
mayonnaise de la mayonnaise [mah-yoh-nayz]
me: he knows me il me [mer] connaît
he saw me il m'a vu
give me . . . donnez-moi . . . [. . . mwah]

give it to me donnez-le moi
it's me c'est moi [say mwah]
meal un repas [rer-pah]
mean: what does this mean? qu'est-ce que ça veut dire? [kesker sah ver deer]
by all means! bien entendu! [bee-yānn ōntōn-doo]
measles la rougeole [roo-johl]
German measles la rubéole [roobay-ohl]
measure mesurer [merzoo-ray]
measurements les dimensions [deemōns-yōn]
meat de la viande [vee-yōnd]
mechanic: is there a mechanic here? est-ce qu'il y a un mécanicien ici? [eskeel-yah ān maykah-nees-yān ee-see]
medical: medical treatment un traitement [trait-mōn]
medicine *(drug)* un remède [rer-maid]
meet rencontrer
I met him last year je l'ai rencontré l'année dernière [jer lay rōnkōn-tray . . .]
when shall we meet? quand est-ce que nous nous voyons? [kōntes-ker noo noo vwah-yōn]
pleased to meet you enchanté(e) de faire votre connaissance [ōnshōn-tay der fair vohtr kohnay-sōns]
meeting une réunion [ray-oon-yōn]
melon un melon [mer-lōn]
member un membre [mōnmbr]
how do I become a member? comment est-ce que je peux devenir membre? [koh-mōnt esker jer per derver-neer . . .]
memories les souvenirs
mend: can you mend this? est-ce que vous pouvez réparer ça? [. . . raypah-ray sah]
mention: don't mention it je vous en prie [jer vooz ōn pree]
menu: can I see the menu, please? est-ce que je peux voir la carte, s'il vous plaît? [esker jer per vwahr lah kart . . .]
we'll have the set menu nous prenons le plat du jour [noo prer-nōn ler plah doo joor]
do you have a set-price menu? est-ce que vous avez un menu touristique? [. . . mer-noo toorees-teek]
» *TRAVEL TIP: see the menu reader pp. 72–73*

mess: my room is in a mess ma chambre est en désordre [. . . o̅n̅ day-zohrdr]
message: are there any messages for me? est-ce qu'il y a une commission pour moi? [eskeel-yah oon kohmees-yo̅n̅ poor mwah]
can I leave a message for . . .? est-ce que je peux laisser un mot pour . . .? [. . . lay-say a̅n̅ moh poor]
messieurs *men*
metre un mètre [maitr]
» *TRAVEL TIP: 1 metre = 39.37 ins = 1.09 yds*

feet	*3.3*	*6.6*	*10*	*16.6*	*33*	*333*
metres	*1*	*2*	*3*	*5*	*10*	*100*

meter un compteur [ko̅n̅-terr]
has the meter been read? est-ce qu'on a relevé le compteur? [esko̅n̅n ah rerl-vay . . .]
métro *underground*
» *TRAVEL TIP: flat fare on whole network of Paris métro; a 'carnet de tickets' (book of 10 tickets) is more economical than single tickets; tickets valid on Paris bus network, but not on 'RER' (Greater Paris fast commuter train)*
midday midi [mee-dee]
at midday à midi
middle le milieu [meel-yer]
in the middle (of) au milieu (de)
midnight minuit [meen-wee]
at midnight à minuit
might: I might be late je serai peut-être en retard [jer ser-ray pert-aitr . . .]
I might come je viendrai peut-être [jer vee-ya̅n̅-dray pert-aitr]
he might have gone il est peut-être parti [eel ay pert-aitr . . .]
migraine une migraine [mee-grain]
mild doux [doo]
mile un mille [meel]
» *TRAVEL TIP: conversion: miles ÷ 5 × 8 = kilometres*

miles	*0.5*	*1*	*3*	*5*	*10*	*50*	*100*
kilometres	*0.8*	*1.6*	*4.8*	*8*	*16*	*80*	*160*

milk du lait [lay]
a glass of milk un verre de lait [vair der lay]
milkshake un milkshake
millimetre un millimètre [meelee-maitr]

Entrées: Starters
Crudités *various salads and raw vegetables*
Terrine du chef *pâté maison*
Oeufs mayonnaise *egg mayonnaise*
Bouchées à la reine *chicken vol-au-vent*

Potages: Soups
Crème de bolets *cream of mushroom*
Velouté de tomates *cream of tomato*
Soupe à l'oignon *onion soup*

Viandes: Meat dishes
Boeuf *beef,* porc *pork,* veau *veal,* agneau *lamb*
Rôti de boeuf *roast beef*
Gigot d'agneau *roast leg of lamb*
Côtelette de porc *pork chop*
Foie de veau *veal liver*
Langue de boeuf *tongue*
Bifteck *steak*
Tournedos *fillet steak*
Escalope panée *slice of veal in breadcrumbs*
Paupiettes de veau *veal olives*
Rognons madère *kidneys in madeira sauce*

Volaille: poultry
Poule au riz *chicken and rice*
Poulet rôti *roast chicken*
Canard à l'orange *duck with orange*

Chasse: game
Civet de lièvre *jugged hare*
Lapin chasseur *rabbit in white wine and herbs*

Poissons et marée: fish and seafood
Coquilles Saint-Jacques *scallops*
Huîtres *oysters*
Moules marinière *mussels in white wine*
Truite aux amandes *trout with almonds*
Raie au beurre noir *skate in black butter*
Homard à l'armoricaine *lobster in white wine sauce with shallots*
Cabillaud *cod,* langouste *crayfish,* langoustine *scampi,* morue *salt cod*

A few menu terms: à l'ail *(with) garlic,* aux câpres *in caper sauce,* à la crème *with cream,* garni *with chips (or rice) and vegetables,* en gelée *in aspic,* provençale *cooked in olive oil with garlic, tomatoes and herbs,* au vin blanc *in white wine,* vinaigrette *sharp vinegar dressing*

Légumes: vegetables

Pommes de terre à l'anglaise *steamed potatoes,* pommes dauphine *potato croquettes,* (pommes) frites *chips,* purée *mashed potatoes*

Chou *cabbage,* chou-fleur *cauliflower,* courgettes *baby marrows,* épinards *spinach,* haricots verts *French beans,* petits pois *peas*

Salads

Salade *green salad with French dressing*

Salade niçoise *with green beans, peppers, anchovies, olives*

Salade russe *mixed vegetable in mayonnaise*

Fromages: le plateau de fromages *cheese board*

Dessert

Glace *ice-cream,* flan *egg custard*

Tarte aux myrtilles *bilberry tart*

Cerises *cherries,* fraises *strawberries,* poire *pear,* pomme *apple,* pêche *peach,* raisin *grapes*

Snacks

Assiette anglaise *cold meats,* saucisse,
frites *Frankfurter sausage and chips,* crêpes *pancakes,*
croque-monsieur *toasted ham and cheese sandwich,*
omelette au jambon/fromage *ham/cheese omelette,*
sandwich aux rillettes *potted meat sandwich*

Wines: *apart from the well-known 'beaujolais' or more expensive 'bourgogne' and 'bordeaux', try 'Côtes du Rhône' (red or white) and Anjou wines (rosé or white)*
sec *dry,* demi-sec *medium dry*

Enjoy your meal! – or, as they say, **bon appétit!**

milometer = le compteur kilométrique [kon-terr keeloh-may-treek]
minced meat de la viande hachée [vee-yond ah-shay]
mind: I've changed my mind j'ai changé d'avis [jay shon-jay dah-vee]
I don't mind ça ne me dérange pas [sahn mer day-ronj pah]
(it's all the same) ça m'est égal [sah mayt ay-gal]
do you mind if I . . .? est-ce que ça vous dérange si . . .? [esker sah voo day-ronj see]
never mind tant pis [ton pee]
mine *see* **my**
mineral water de l'eau minérale [oh meenay-rahl]
minimum le minimum [meenee-mom]
the minimum charge le tarif minimum
minus moins [mwan]
minute une minute [mee-noot]
in a minute dans un instant [donz an ans-ton]
just a minute un instant
mirror une glace [glahs]
(rear view) le rétroviseur [raytroh-vee-zerr]
Miss Mademoiselle [mahd-mwah-zel]
miss: we missed the train/boat nous avons manqué le train/bateau [nooz ah-von mon-kay . . .]
I miss you vous me manquez [voo mer mon-kay]
my wallet/sister is missing mon portefeuille/ma soeur a disparu [. . . ah deespah-roo]
there's something/there are 2 people missing il y a quelque chose qui manque/deux personnes qui manquent [eelyah kelker-shohz . . . kee monk]
mist la brume [broom]
mistake une erreur [ay-rerr]
I think you've made a mistake je crois que vous vous êtes trompé [jer krwah ker voo vooz ait tron-pay]
misunderstanding: there's been a misunderstanding il y a eu un malentendu [eelyah oo an mahlon-ton-doo]
mix mélanger [maylon-jay]
modern moderne [moh-dairn]
moisturizer une lotion hydratante [lohs-yon eedrah-tont]
moment un moment [moh-mon]
Monday lundi [lan-dee]

money: I've lost my money j'ai perdu mon argent [jay pair-doo mōn ahr-jōn]
I have no money je n'ai pas d'argent [jer nay pah dahr-jōn]
» *TRAVEL TIP: French currency*
The unit is 'un franc', divided up into 100 'centimes'; main coins are 10 centimes, 20c, 50c, 1F, 2F, 5F and 10F; the 10F coin is easily mistaken for other large coins; main notes are 10F, 20F, 50F, 100F, 500F
month un mois [mwah]
monument un monument [mohnoo-mōn]
moon la lune [loon]
moorings *(ropes)* les amarres [ah-mahr]
moped un cyclomoteur [seekloh-moh-terr]
more plus [ploo(s)]
more expensive (than) plus cher (que) [ploo shair ker]
more people/money plus de gens/d'argent [ploos der . . .]
can I have some more? est-ce que je peux en avoir plus? [. . . ōnn ah-vwahr ploos]
more wine, please encore du vin, s'il vous plaît [ōn-kor doo vān . . .]
no more, thank you merci, ça suffit [mair-see sah soo-fee]
no more money plus [ploo] d'argent
I haven't got any more je n'en ai plus [jer nōnn ay ploo]
there aren't any more il n'y en a plus [eeln yōnn ah ploo]
morning le matin [mah-tān]
in the morning le matin
the following morning le lendemain matin [lōnd-mān mah-tān]
mosquito un moustique [moos-teek]
most: the most . . . le plus . . . [ler ploo]
I like this one the most c'est celui-ci que je préfère [say ser-lwee-see ker jer pray-fair]
most of the time/the people la plupart du temps/des gens [lah ploo-par doo tōn, day jōn]
that's most kind c'est très gentil [say tray jōn-tee]
motel un motel [moh-tel]
mother: my mother ma mère [mair]

motor le moteur [moh-ter]
motorbike une moto [moh-toh]
motorboat un canot automobile [kah-noh ohtoh-moh-beel]
motorcyclist un motocycliste [mohtoh-see-kleest]
motorist un automobiliste [ohtoh-moh-bee-leest]
motorway l'autoroute [ohtoh-root]
» *TRAVEL TIP: toll motorways in France (relatively expensive); you either pay at the 'péage' (toll-station) or get a card there and pay on exit; most M-ways are 2-lane only: be extra careful where lanes merge; the Paris ring road ('le périphérique') is toll-free*
mountain une montagne [mōn-tan]
in the mountains à la montagne
mountaineering l'alpinisme [alpee-neesm]
mouse une souris [soo-ree]
moustache une moustache [moos-tahsh]
mouth la bouche [boosh]
move bouger [boo-jay]
don't move ne bougez pas [ner boo-jay pah]
could you move your car? est-ce que vous pouvez déplacer votre voiture? [. . . dayplah-say vohtr vwah-toor]
Mrs Madame [mah-dam], Mme
Ms *no equivalent in French*
much beaucoup [boh-koo]
much better/much more beaucoup mieux/plus
not much pas beaucoup [pah . . .]
mug: I've been mugged j'ai été attaqué [ahtah-kay]
coffee mug une grande tasse [grōnd tahs]
muscle un muscle [mooskl]
I've strained a muscle je me suis claqué un muscle [jer mer swee klah-kay . . .]
museum un musée [moo-zay]
» *TRAVEL TIP: most museums and castles are closed on Tuesdays in France*
mushroom un champignon [shōnpeen-yōn]
music la musique [moo-zeek]
mussels des moules [mool]
must devoir [der-vwahr]
I must go je dois partir [jer dwah . . .]
we must not . . . nous ne devons pas . . . [noo ner der-vōn pah]

you must . . . vous devez . . . [voo der-vay]
mustard de la moutarde
mutton du mouton [moo-ton]
my mon [mon], ma [mah], *(plural)* mes [may]
it's my bag, it's mine c'est mon sac, c'est le mien [. . . ler mee-yan]
it's my car, it's mine c'est ma voiture, c'est la mienne [. . . lah mee-yen] *(plural:* 'les miens, les miennes')
nail *(on finger)* un ongle [ongl]
(in wood etc) un clou [kloo]
nail clippers une pince à ongles [pans . . .]
nail file une lime à ongles [leem . . .]
nail polish du vernis à ongles [vair-nee . . .]
nail scissors des ciseaux à ongles [see-zoh . . .]
naked nu [noo]
name un nom [non]
my name is . . . je m'appelle . . . [jer mah-pel]
what's your name? quel est votre nom? [kel-ay vohtr non]
what's the name of . . .? comment s'appelle . . .? [koh-mon sah-pel]
napkin une serviette [sairv-yet]
nappies les couches [koosh]
disposable nappies des couches à jeter [. . . ah jer-tay]
nappy liners les protège-couches [proh-tayj-koosh]
narrow étroit [ay-trwah]
national national [nahs-yoh-nal]
nationality la nationalité [nahs-yoh-nah-lee-tay]
natural naturel [nahtoo-rel]
naughty: don't be naughty soyez sage [swah-yay sahj]
near: is it near? est-ce que c'est près? [esker say pray]
near here/home près d'ici/de chez nous [pray dee-see, der shay noo]
where's the nearest chemist/bank? où est la pharmacie/banque la plus proche? [oo ay . . . lah ploo prosh]
do you go near . . .? est-ce que vous passez près de . . .? [. . . pah-say pray der]
nearly presque [presk]
neat *(drink)* sec

necessary nécessaire [naysay-sair]
neck le cou [koo]
necklace le collier [kol-yay]
need: I need a . . . j'ai besoin d'un . . . [jay ber-zwān]
  he needs . . . il a besoin de . . .
  I/we need to leave je dois/nous devons partir [jer dwah, noo der-vōn . . .]
needle une aiguille [ay-gwee]
negative *(photo)* un négatif [naygah-teef]
neighbour un voisin [vwah-zān]
neither: neither of them aucun des deux [oh-kān day der]
  neither I nor . . . ni moi ni . . . [nee mwah nee]
  neither do I moi non plus [mwah nōn ploo]
nephew: my nephew mon neveu [ner-ver]
nervous nerveux [nair-ver]
net: net price le prix net [pree net]
nettoyage à sec *dry cleaning*
never jamais [jah-may]
  I've never been there je n'y suis jamais allé [jer nee swee jah-may ah-lay]
new nouveau [noo-voh]
  (not used) neuf [nerf]
news les nouvelles [noo-vel]
  newsagent un kiosque à journaux [kee-yosk ah joor-noh]
  newspaper un journal [joor-nal]
  do you have any English newspapers?
  est-ce que vous avez des journaux anglais? [. . . day joor-noh ōn-glay]
New Year la nouvelle année [noo-vel ah-nay]
  on New Year's day le jour de l'An [ler joor der lōn]
» *TRAVEL TIP: usually an occasion for a big meal with friends, 'le réveillon'* [rayvay-yōn]
  on New Year's Eve à la Saint Sylvestre [ah lah sān seel-vaistr]
  happy New Year bonne année [bon ah-nay]
New Zealand la Nouvelle Zélande [noo-vel zay-lōnd]
next *(bus, train)* prochain [pro-shān]
  next to . . . à côté de . . . [ah koh-tay der]
  stop at the next corner arrêtez-vous au prochain croisement
  [ahray-tay voo oh proh-shān krwahz-mōn]

see you next year! à l'année prochaine! [ah lay-nay proh-shan̄]
next week la semaine prochaine [lah ser-main proh-shan̄]
when is the next train? quand part le prochain train? [kon̄ par ler proh-shan̄. . .]
where is the next stop? où est le prochain arrêt? [oo ay ler proh-shain ah-ray]
nice *(nice-looking)* joli [joh-lee]
(pleasant, kind) gentil [jon̄-tee]
niece: my niece ma nièce [nee-yes]
night la nuit [nwee]
at night la nuit
night club un night-club
night-dress une chemise de nuit [sher-meez . . .]
night porter le portier de nuit [pohrt-yay . . .]
no *(reply)* non [non̄]
there's no water/toilet paper il n'y a pas d'eau/de papier hygiénique [eelnyah pah der . . .]
I've no money je n'ai pas d'argent [jer nay pah . . .]
nobody personne [pair-son]
nobody saw him personne ne l'a vu [pair-son ner . . .]
noise le bruit [brwee]
it's very noisy il y a beaucoup de bruit
our room is too noisy notre chambre est trop bruyante [nohtr shon̄br ay troh brwee-yon̄t]
none aucun [oh-kan̄]
none of them aucun d'entre eux [. . . don̄tr er]
nonsense: I don't want any nonsense je ne veux pas d'histoires [jern ver pah dees-twahr]
non-smoker non-fumeurs [non̄ foo-mer]
noon: at noon à midi [mee-dee]
normal normal [nohr-mal]
north le nord [nor]
North America l'Amérique du Nord [ahmay-reek doo nor]
Northern Ireland l'Irlande du Nord [eer-lon̄d doo nor]
nose le nez [nay]
I have a nosebleed je saigne du nez [jer sayn . . .]
not pas [pah]
not me/that one pas moi/celui-là
I'm not hungry je n'ai pas faim [jer nay pah . . .]

he's not here il n'est pas là [eel nay pah . . .]
I don't want . . . je ne veux pas . . . [jer ner ver pah]
he doesn't understand il ne comprend pas [eel ner . . . pah]
I didn't . . . je n'ai pas . . .
he didn't tell me il ne m'a pas dit
there isn't any . . . il n'y a pas de . . .
note *(bank note)* un billet (de banque) [bee-yay der bonk]
notepaper du papier à lettres [pahp-yay ah laitr]
nothing rien [ree-yan]
there's nothing il n'y a rien
notice: I didn't notice (that) . . . je n'ai pas remarqué (que) . . . [jer nay pah rermahr-kay ker]
November: in November en novembre [noh-vonbr]
now maintenant [mant-non]
nowhere nulle part [nool par]
nudist un nudiste [noo-deest]
nudist beach une plage réservée aux nudistes
nuisance: it's a nuisance c'est ennuyeux [sayt on-nwee-yer]
he's being a nuisance il nous importune [eel nooz anpor-toon]
numb engourdi [ongoor-dee]
number le numéro [noomay-roh]
(quantity) le nombre [nonbr]
number plates les plaques d'immatriculation [plak deemah-tree-koo-lahs-yon]
nurse une infirmière [anfeerm-yair]
nursery slope une piste pour débutants [peest poor dayboo-ton]
nut *(for bolt)* un écrou [ay-kroo]
(to eat) no single general term: be specific see **peanuts**
nylon du nylon [nee-lon]
oar une rame [rahm]
objets trouvés *lost property*
obligatory obligatoire [ohblee-gah-twahr]
obvious: it's obvious c'est évident [set ayvee-don]
occasionally de temps en temps [der tonz on ton]
occupied: is this seat occupied? est-ce que cette place est prise? [. . . set plass ay preez]
o'clock *see* **time**

October: in October en octobre [onn ok-tohbr]
octopus un poulpe [poolp]
odd *(strange)* bizarre
odd number un nombre impair [nonbr an-pair]
off: the milk is off le lait a tourné [. . . ah toor-nay]
this meat is off cette viande n'est plus bonne [. . . ploo bon]
10% off dix pour cent de réduction [dee poor son der raydooks-yon]
it came off c'est tombé [say ton-bay]
can you switch it off? est-ce que vous pouvez l'éteindre? [. . . ay-tandr]
offence un délit [day-lee]
offensive injurieux [anjoor-yer]
offer: can I offer you . . .? puis-je vous offrir . . .? [pweej vooz oh-freer]
office un bureau [boo-roh]
officer *(to policeman)* Monsieur l'agent [mers-yer lah-jon]
official officiel [ohfees-yel]
(person) un employé [onplwah-yay]
often souvent [soo-von]
oil de l'huile [weel]
(cooking) de l'huile comestible [kohmes-teebl]
(petroleum) du pétrole [pay-trol]
I'm losing oil je perds [pair] de l'huile
will you change the oil? est-ce que vous pouvez me faire une vidange? [. . . mer fair oon vee-donj]
ointment une pommade [poh-mad]
O.K. d'accord [dah-kor]
it's O.K. ça va [sah vah]
old vieux (vieille) [vee-yer, vee-yay]
how old are you? quel âge avez-vous? [kel ahj ah-vay voo]
olive une olive [oh-leev]
green/black olives des olives vertes/noires [. . . vairt, nwahr]
omelette une omelette
cheese/ham omelette une omelette au fromage/jambon [ohm-let oh froh-mahj, jon-bon]
on sur [soor]
I haven't got it on me je ne l'ai pas sur moi [jer ner lay pah soor mwah]

put the light on allumez la lumière [ahloo-may . . .]
on Monday etc lundi etc
on Mondays etc le lundi etc
on television à la télévision
once une fois [oon fwah]
at once tout de suite [toot sweet]
one un (une) [an, oon]
the red one le (la) rouge
one way street une rue à sens unique [roo ah sons oo-neek]
onion un oignon [ohn-yon]
only seulement [serl-mon]
open ouvert [oo-vair]
when do you open? quand est-ce que vous ouvrez? [kont esker vooz oo-vray]
I can't open it je n'arrive pas à l'ouvrir [jer nah-reev pah ah loo-vreer]
open return un billet de retour 'open' [bee-yay der rer-toor . . .]
opera un opéra [ohpay-rah]
opera house l'opéra
operation une opération [ohpay-rahs-yon]
will I need an operation? est-ce qu'il faudra m'opérer? [eskeel foh-drah mohpay-ray]
operator *(telephone)* l'opératrice [ohpay-rah-trees]
» TRAVEL TIP: dial 10 to call the operator, and 12 ('renseignements') for international calls and enquiries
opposite en face (de) [on fahs der]
optician un opticien [optees-yan]
or ou [oo]
orange une orange [oh-ronj]
orange juice un jus [joo] d'orange
orchestra un orchestre [ohr-kestr]
order: could we order now? est-ce qu'on peut commander maintenant? [eskon per kohmon-day mant-non]
thank you, we've already ordered merci, nous avons déjà commandé
it's out of order ça ne marche pas [sah ner marsh pah]
original original [ohree-jee-nal]
other autre [ohtr]

the other one l'autre
do you have any others? est-ce que vous en avez d'autres?
otherwise autrement [ohtrer-mōn]
ought: I ought to go je devrais partir [jer der-vray par-teer]
ounce *1 ounce = 28.35 grammes*
our notre [nohtr], nos [noh]
our car/son notre voiture/fils
our tickets/cars nos billets/voitures
it's ours c'est le (la) nôtre [ler, lah nohtr]
these are ours ce sont les nôtres [lay nohtr]
out dehors [der-ohr]
we're out of petrol nous n'avons plus d'essence [noo nah-vōn ploo . . .]
outboard un hors-bord [ohr-bohr]
outdoors dehors [der-ohr]
outside dehors [der-ohr]
can we sit outside? est-ce qu'on peut se mettre dehors?
ouvert *open*
over: over here ici [ee-see]
over there là-bas [lah-bah]
he's over 40 il a plus de [ploo der] quarante ans
it's all over c'est fini [say fee-nee]
overboard: man overboard! un homme à la mer! [ānn om ah lah mair]
overcharge: you've overcharged me la facture est trop élevée [lah fak-toor ay trohp ayl-vay]
overcooked trop cuit [troh kwee]
overexposed surexposé [soorex-poh-zay]
overnight la nuit [nwee]
we want to stay overnight nous voulons passer la nuit ici [. . . pah-say la nwee . . .]
oversleep: I overslept j'a dormi trop longtemps [jay dor-mee troh lōn-tōn]
overtake dépasser [daypah-say]
owe: what do I/we owe you? combien est-ce que je vous dois/nous vous devons? [kōnb-yān esker jer voo dwah, noo voo der-vōn]
you owe me 10F vous me devez dix francs [voo mer der-vay]
own: my own . . . mon propre . . . [prohpr]

I'm on my own je suis seul [jer swee serl]
owner le propriétaire [prohpree-yay-tair]
oxygen l'oxygène [oxee-jen]
oysters des huîtres [weetr]
pack: I haven't packed yet je n'ai pas encore fait mes bagages
[jer nay pahz on-kot fay may bah-gahj]
can I have a packed lunch? est-ce que je peux avoir un pique-nique? [. . . peek-neek]
package tour un voyage organisé [voh-yahj orgah-nee-zay]
packet: a packet of . . . un paquet de . . . [pah-kay]
padlock un verrou [vay-roo]
page la page [pahj]
could you page him? est-ce que vous pouvez le faire appeler? [. . . ler fair ap-lay]
pain: I've got a pain here j'ai mal ici
[jay mal ee-see]
I've got a pain in my leg/back j'ai mal à la jambe/aux reins
painkillers des calmants [kal-mon]
painful douloureux [dooloo-rer]
painting un tableau [tah-bloh]
pair: pair of gloves/shoes une paire de gants/chaussures [pair der . . .]
pale pâle [pahl]
pancake une crêpe [kraip]
panties un slip
pants *(underpants)* un slip
(trousers) un pantalon [pontah-lon]
paper *(newspaper)* un journal [joor-nal]
a piece of paper un (morceau de) papier [mohr-soh der pahp-yay]
paper hankies des mouchoirs en papier [moo-shwahr . . .]
paraffin *paraffin oil is not used in France for domestic purposes*
parcel un colis [koh-lee]
pardon *(I didn't understand)* pardon . . . [pahr-don]
I beg your pardon *(sorry)* excusez-moi [exkoo-zay mwah]
parents: my parents mes parents [pah-ron]
Paris Paris [pah-ree]

park *(noun)* un parc
where can I park my car? où est-ce que je peux garer ma voiture? [wesker jer per gah-ray mah vwah-toor]
» *TRAVEL TIP: disc zones in most towns: you must display a 'disque de stationnement' (parking disc) on your windscreen; for further information go to the local 'syndicat d'initiative' (tourist office)*
part: part of une partie de [pahr-tee der]
(spare) part une pièce de rechange [pee-yes der rer-shōnj]
partner *(business)* un associé [ahsohs-yay]
(games) un partenaire [parter-nair]
party *(group)* un groupe [groop]
(celebration) une réunion [ray-oon-yōn]
(in the evening) une soirée [swah-ray]
I'm with the English party je suis avec le groupe anglais
pass *(mountain)* un col
he's passed out il s'est évanoui [eel sayt ayvah-nwee]
passable *(road)* praticable [prah-tee-kahbl]
passage souterrain *subway*
passage protégé *stretch of main road where traffic coming from the side roads doesn't have right of way*
passenger un passager [pahsah-jay]
passer-by un passant [pah-sōn]
passport: my passport mon passeport [pass-pohr]
past: in the past autrefois [ohtr-fwah]
do you go past the station? est-ce que vous passez devant la gare? [esker voo pah-say der-vōn . . .]
pasta des pâtes [paht]
pastry de la pâtisserie [pahtees-ree]
path un chemin [sher-mān]
patient: be patient soyez patient [swah-yay pahs-yōn]
pâtisserie *baker's*
pattern *(design)* un dessin [day-sān]
pavement le trottoir [troh-twahr]
pay *(verb)* payer [pay-yay]
can I pay, please? est-ce que je peux payer, s'il vous plaît?
PCV: communication en PCV *reverse charge call*
pea: peas des petits pois [per-tee pwah]

peace la paix [pay]
peach une pêche [pesh]
péage *toll*
peanuts: salted peanuts des cacahuètes salées [kahkah-wet sah-lay]
pear une poire [pwahr]
pebble un galet [gah-lay]
pedal la pédale [pay-dahl]
pedestrian un piéton [pee-yay-ton]
pedestrian crossing un passage pour piétons [pah-sahj . . .]
» *TRAVEL TIP: do not assume that cars will stop or even slow down once you are on a pedestrian crossing; be extra cautious, especially with children*
peg *(for tent)* un piquet de tente [pee-kay der tont] *(clothes)* une pince à linge [pans ah lanj]
pelvis le bassin [bah-san]
pen: have you got a pen? est-ce que vous avez un stylo? [. . . stee-loh]
pencil un crayon [kray-yon]
penfriend un correspondant [kohres-pon-don]
penicillin la pénicilline [paynee-see-leen]
penknife un canif [kah-neef]
pension *guesthouse*
pensioner un retraité [rertray-tay]
people les gens [jon]
how many people? combien de personnes? [pair-son]
pepper du poivre [pwahvr]
green/red peppers des poivrons verts/rouges [pwah-vron vair, rooj]
peppermint une pastille de menthe [pahs-tee der mont]
per: per cent pour cent [poor son]
per day/week/person par jour/semaine/personne
perfect parfait [par-fay]
the perfect holiday des vacances idéales [vah-kons eeday-ahl]
performance *(theatre etc)* une représentation [rerpray-zon-tahs-yon]
perfume un parfum [pahr-fan]
perhaps peut-être [per-taitr]
périphérique *'le périphérique' is the Paris ring road*
period *(menstruation)* les règles [raygl] *(time)* une période [payr-yod]

perm une permanente [pairmah-nont]
permanent permanent [pairmah-non]
permit un permis [pair-mee]
permission une permission [pairmees-yon]
person une personne [pair-son]
in person en personne
personal personnel [pairsoh-nel]
for personal use à usage personnel
I'd like to make a personal call j'aimerais une communication avec préavis [. . . kohmoo-nee-kahs-yon ah-vek pray-ah-vee]
pet un animal domestique [ahnee-mal dohmes-teek]
petrol de l'essence [ay-sons]
petrol station une station-service [stahs-yon-sair-vees]
petrol gauge la jauge [johj] à essence
petrol can le jerrycan d'essence
petrol tank le réservoir
YOU MAY SEE OR HEAR . . .
super [soo-pair] = *4-star*
ordinaire [ohrdee-nair] = *2-star*
normale [nor-mahl] = *2-star*
give me 50F worth of 4-star donnez-moi pour cinquante francs de super [doh-nay-mwah poor san-kont fron der soo-pair]
» *TRAVEL TIP: the pump attendant will expect a tip if he gives your windscreen a wipe; routine checks such as 'les niveaux' (oil and battery level) can be costly*
phone *see* **telephone**
photograph une photo
would you take a photograph of us? est-ce que vous pouvez nous prendre en photo? [esker voo poo-vay noo prondr on fohtoh]
piano un piano
pickpocket un pickpocket
picture *(photo)* une photo
picnic un pique-nique [peek-neek]
pie: pork pie un pâté en croûte [pah-tay on kroot]
» *TRAVEL TIP: pies as you know them do not exist in France; for a snack buy sandwiches in a café (look for the sign 'casse-croûte'), or buy bread (a 'baguette') and ham, pâté etc for a tasty 'pique-nique'*

piece: a piece of . . . un morceau de . . . [mohr-soh]
piétons *pedestrians*
pig un cochon [koh-shon]
pigeon un pigeon [pee-jon]
pile-up une collision en chaîne [kohleez-yon . . .]
pill: do you take the pill? est-ce que vous prenez la pilule? [esker voo prer-nay lah pee-lool]
pillion: on the pillion sur le siège arrière [soor ler see-yej ahr-yair]
pillow un oreiller [ohray-yay]
pin une épingle [ay-pangl]
pineapple un ananas [ahnah-nas]
pink rose [rohz]
pint = *approx.* un demi-litre [dermee-leetr]
» *TRAVEL TIP: 1 pint = 0.57 litre; if you ask for a beer, the standard measure is 0.33 l, slightly more than a half-pint (0.26 l)*
pipe une pipe [peep]
(for water) un tuyau [twee-yoh]
pipe tobacco du tabac [tah-bah] pour la pipe
piston un piston [pees-ton]
pity: it's a pity! c'est dommage! [doh-mahj]
place: is this place taken? est-ce que cette place [plahs] est prise?
do you know any good places to go? est-ce que vous connaissez des endroits [an-drwah] intéressants?
places debout *standing room*
places assises *seated accommodation*
plain simple [sanpl]
plain omelette une omelette nature [. . . nah-toor]
plain fabric du tissu uni [. . . oo-nee]
plan: we plan to . . . nous avons l'intention de . . . [nooz ah-von lantons-yon der]
plane un avion [ahv-yon]
plant *(flower etc)* une plante [plont]
(factory) une usine [oo-zeen]
plaster *(cast)* un plâtre [plahtr]
plastic: plastic bag un sac en plastique [sak on plahs-teek]
plate une assiette [ahs-yet]
platform: which platform? quel quai? [kel kay]
play jouer [joo-ay]
somewhere for the children to play un endroit où

les enfants peuvent jouer [ānn ōn-drwah oo layz ōnfōn perv joo-ay]
pleasant agréable [ahgray-ahbl]
please s'il vous plaît [seel voo play]
could you please . . .? s'il vous plaît, est-ce que vous pouvez . . .? [. . . esker voo poo-vay]
yes please oui, s'il vous plaît
I am pleased to/with . . . je suis content de . . . [jer swee kōn-tōn der]
pleasure: it's a pleasure bien volontiers [bee-yān vohlōnt-yay]
with pleasure avec plaisir [ah-vek play-zeer]
plenty: plenty of . . . beaucoup de . . . [boh-koo der]
thank you, that's plenty merci, ça suffit [. . . sah soo-fee]
pliers des tenailles [ter-nah-ee]
plug *(electrical)* une prise [preez]
(car) une bougie [boo-jee]
(sink etc) la bonde [bōnd]
plum une prune [proon]
plumber un plombier [plōnb-yay]
plumbing la plomberie [plōn-bree]
plus plus [ploos]
p.m.: 1 p.m. une heure de l'après-midi [oon err der lah-pray-mee-dee]
7 p.m. sept heures du soir [set err doo swahr]
pneumonia une pneumonie [pnermoh-nee]
poached egg un oeuf poché [erf poh-shay]
pocket une poche [posh]
poids lourds *heavy goods vehicles*
point: could you point to it? est-ce que vous pouvez me l'indiquer? [. . . āndee-kay]
four point six quatre virgule six [. . . veer-gool . . .]
points *(car)* les vis platinées [vees plahtee-nay]
police la police [poh-lees]
get the police! appelez la police! [ap-lay . . .]
policeman un agent de police [ah-jōn der poh-lees]
police station le commissariat [kohmee-sahr-yah]
YOU MAY SEE . . .
gendarmerie *police station (the 'gendarmes' operate outside large cities and on the roads)*
polish *(for shoes)* du cirage [see-rahj]

could you polish my shoes? est-ce que vous pouvez cirer mes souliers? [. . . see-ray may sool-yay]
polite poli [poh-lee]
politics la politique
polluted pollué [pohloo-ay]
polythene bag un sac en plastique
pool *(swimming)* une piscine [pee-seen]
poor pauvre [pohvr]
(quality) médiocre [maid-yohkr]
popular populaire [pohpoo-lair]
is it popular? *(place)* est-ce que c'est très fréquenté? [esker say tray frayko̅n̅-tay]
population la population [pohpoo-lahs-yo̅n̅]
pork du porc [pohr]
port *(harbour)* un port [pohr]
(drink) du porto
to port à bâbord [ah bah-bohr]
porter un porteur [por-terr]
portrait un portrait [por-tray]
posh chic
possible possible [poh-seebl]
could you possibly . . .? est-ce que vous pourriez . . .? [esker voo poor-yay]
post *(a letter)* poster [pohs-tay]
what's the postage for . . .? il faut affranchir à combien pour . . .? [eel foh ahfro̅n̅-sheer ah ko̅n̅b-ya̅n̅ poor]
post box une boîte aux lettres [bwaht oh laitr]
postcard une carte postale [. . . .pohs-tahl]
post office la poste
poste restante la poste restante [pohst res-to̅n̅t]
» *TRAVEL TIP: you can telephone from any post office (open 8 am to 7 pm and 8–12 Sat mornings); in Paris the main post office is open 24 hrs a day, 7 days a week: 52 rue du Louvre; letter boxes are yellow; you may be asked to show your passport when collecting 'poste restante' items*
YOU MAY SEE . . .
colis *parcels*
timbres *stamps*
poster un poster [pos-tair]
postman le facteur [fak-terr]
potato une pomme de terre [pom der tair]

pottery une poterie [pot-ree]
pound une livre [leevr]; *NB: the 'livre' is 500g*
» *TRAVEL TIP: conversion: pounds ÷ 11 × 5 = kilos*

pounds	*1*	*3*	*5*	*6*	*7*	*8*	*9*
kilos	*0.4*	*1.4*	*2.3*	*2.7*	*3.2*	*3.6*	*4.1*

poussez *push*
pour verser [vair-say]
it's pouring il pleut à verse [eel pler ah vairs]
powder la poudre [poodr]
powdered milk du lait en poudre
power cut une panne d'électricité [pan daylek-tree-see-tay]
power point une prise de courant [preez der koo-ron]
prawns des crevettes roses [krer-vet rohz]
prawn cocktail un cocktail de crevettes
prefer: I prefer ... je préfère ... [jer pray-fair]
pregnant: she is pregnant elle est enceinte [el ayt on-sant]
prepare préparer [praypah-ray]
prescription: can you make up this prescription? est-ce que vous pouvez préparer cette ordonnance? [... praypah-ray set ohrdoh-nons]
present: at present à présent [ah pray-zon]
here's a present for ... voilà un cadeau pour ... [vwahla an kah-doh poor]
it's for a present c'est pour offrir [say poor oh-freer]
president le président [prayzee-don]
press: could you press these? est-ce que vous pouvez repasser ces vêtements? [rerpah-say say vait-mon]
pressing *dry cleaning*
pressure la pression [prays-yon]
prêt-à-porter *ready-to-wear*
pretty joli [joh-lee]
pretty expensive assez cher [ah-say ...]
price le prix [pree]
price list le tarif [tah-reef]
prière de ... *please ...*
priest un prêtre [praitr]
primeurs *early produce*
print *(photo)* une épreuve sur papier [ay-prerv soor pahp-yay]
one print of each une épreuve de chaque [... shahk]
printed matter des imprimés [anpree-may]

priorité (à droite) *right of way (to vehicles coming from the right)*
prison une prison [pree-zōn]
private: private beach/road plage/route privée [. . . pree-vay]
probably probablement [prohbah-bler-mōn]
problem un problème [proh-blem]
product un produit [proh-dwee]
profit un bénéfice [baynay-fees]
programme un programme
(on radio, TV) une émission [aymees-yōn]
promise: I promise that . . . je promets que . . . [jer proh-may ker]
pronounce: how do you pronounce that? comment est-ce que ça se prononce? [koh-mōnt esker sah ser proh-nōns]
propeller une hélice [ay-lees]
properly correctement [kohrek-ter-mōn]
property: it's my property ça m'appartient [sah mahpart-yān]
propriété privée *private, no trespassing*
protect protéger [prohtay-jay]
Protestant protestant [prohtes-tōn]
proud fier [fee-yair]
prove: I can prove it je peux le prouver [jer per ler proo-vay]
PTT *Post Office*
public: the public le public [poo-bleek]
public convenience des toilettes [twah-let] publiques
» *TRAVEL TIP: public toilets are sometimes scarce and difficult to find; remember that cafés and bars always provide such facilities*
public holidays les jours fériés [joor fayr-yay]
» *TRAVEL TIP: public holidays: Jan 1st; Easter; May 1st; Ascension Day; Whitsun and Monday; July 14th ('fête nationale'); Aug 15th ('l'Assomption'); Nov 1st ('la Toussaint'); Nov 11th (Remembrance Day); Dec 25th*
pudding un dessert [day-sair]
pull *(verb)* tirer [tee-ray]
he pulled out in front of me il a déboîté juste devant moi [eel ah daybwah-tay joost der-vōn mwah]

pump une pompe [pōnp]
punctual ponctuel [pōnktoo-el]
puncture: I've had a puncture j'ai eu une crevaison [. . . krervay-zōn]
pure pur [poor]
purple violet [vee-yoh-let]
purpose: on purpose exprès [ex-pray]
purse un porte-monnaie [port-moh-nay]
push pousser [poo-say]
  push chair une poussette [poo-set]
put: where can I put . . .? où est-ce que je peux mettre . . .? [wesker jer per maitr]
  where have you put it? où est-ce que vous l'avez mis? [wesker voo lah-vay mee]
pyjamas pyjamas [peejah-mah]
quai *at station: platform*
quality la qualité [kahlee-tay]
quarantine: to stay in quarantine rester en quarantaine [. . . kahrōn-ten]
quarter: a quarter of an hour un quart d'heure [kahr-der]
quay un quai [kay]
question une question [kest-yōn]
queue une file d'attente [feel dah-tōnt]
» *TRAVEL TIP: don't necessarily expect orderly queuing*
quick rapide [rah-peed]
  that was quick c'était vite fait [say-tay veet fay]
  quickly rapidement [rahpeed-mōn]
quiet tranquille [trōn-keel]
  be quiet! ne faites pas de bruit [ner fait pah der brwee]
quite *(fairly)* assez [ah-say]; *(very)* très [tray]
race une course [koors]
radiator un radiateur [rahd-yah-terr]
radio: on the radio à la radio [rahd-yoh]
rail: by rail en train [ōn trān]
rain la pluie [plwee]
  it's raining il pleut [pler]
  raincoat un imperméable [ānpair-may-ahbl]
ralentir *slow down*
rally *(car)* un rallye [rah-lee]
rape: I've been raped on m'a violée [ōn mah vee-yoh-lay]

rappel *on traffic signs: reminder*
rare rare [rahr]
(steak) saignant [sayn-yoñ]
rarely rarement [rahr-moñ]
rash une éruption de boutons [ayroops-yoñ der boo-toñ]
raspberries des framboises [froñ-bwahz]
rat un rat [rah]
rate: do you have a special rate for children/students? est-ce que vous avez un tarif réduit pour les enfants/étudiants? [... añ tah-reef ray-dwee ...]
what's the rate for sterling? quel est le taux de la livre? [... toh der lah leevr]
rather *(fairly)* assez [ah-say]
I'd rather je préférerais [pray-fair-ray]
raw cru [kroo]
razor un rasoir [rah-zwahr]
razor blades des lames de rasoir [lahm ...]
read: something to read quelque chose à lire [kel-ker shohz ah leer]
would you read this for me? est-ce que vous pouvez me lire ça? [... mer leer sah]
ready: when will it be ready? ce sera prêt quand? [ser serah pray koñ]
I'm not ready yet je ne suis pas encore prêt [jer ner swee pahz oñ-kor pray]
real *(leather etc)* véritable [vayree-tahbl]
really? vraiment? [vray-moñ]
rear-view mirror le rétroviseur [raytroh-vee-zerr]
reasonable raisonnable [rayzoh-nahbl]
receipt: can I have a receipt? est-ce que je peux avoir une quittance? [... kee-toñs]
receive recevoir [rerser-vwahr]
recently récemment [raysah-moñ]
reception *(hotel)* la réception [rayseps-yoñ]
at reception à la réception
receptionist la réceptionniste [rayseps-yoh-neest]
recipe une recette [rer-set]
recommend: can you recommend ...? est-ce que vous pouvez recommander ...? [... rerkoh-moñ-day]
record *(music)* un disque [deesk]
red rouge [rooj]
reduction une réduction [raydooks-yoñ]

refill une recharge [rer-shahrj]
refuse: I refuse . . . je refuse . . . [jer rer-fooz]
region: in this region dans cette région [don set rayj-yon]
registered: I'd like to send this registered j'aimerais envoyer ça en recommandé [jaym-ray onvwah-yay sah on rerkoh-mon-day]
remain rester [res-tay]
remember: do you remember? est-ce que vous vous rappelez? [esker voo voo rap-lay]
I don't remember je ne me rappelle pas [jer ner mer rah-pel pah]
renseignements *enquiries*
rent: can I rent a car/bicycle? est-ce que je peux louer une voiture/bicyclette? [esker jer per loo-ay . . .]
YOU MAY HEAR . . .
une taxe kilométrique [tax keeloh-may-treek] = *mileage charge*
repair: can you repair it? est-ce que vous pouvez le réparer? [. . . ler raypah-ray]
repeat: could you repeat that slowly? est-ce que vous pouvez répéter lentement? [. . . raypay-tay lont-mon]
replace *(give another)* remplacer [ronplah-say]
reply une réponse [ray-pons]
R.E.R. [air-er-air] *fast commuter train in the Greater Paris area*
rescue sauver [soh-vay]
reservation une réservation [rayzair-vahs-yon]
reserve: can I reserve a seat? est-ce que je peux réserver une place? [esker jer per rayzair vay oon plahs]
responsible responsable [respon-sahbl]
rest: the rest of le reste de [rest]
I've come here for a rest je suis venu ici pour me reposer [. . . mer rerpoh-zay]
restaurant un restaurant [restoh-ron]
» *TRAVEL TIP: it often pays to look for a place off the main road or high street; see the menu reader, pp 72–73*
retail price le prix de détail [pree der day-tah-ee]
retired: I am retired je suis à la retraite [jer sweez ah lah rer-trait]
return retourner [rertoor-nay]

a return/two returns to . . . un/deux aller-retour pour . . . [. . . ahlay rer-toor poor]
reverse gear la marche arrière [marsh ahr-yair]
reverse charge call une communication en PCV [kohmoo-nee-kahs-yo̅n̅ o̅n̅ pay-say-vay]
rez-de-chaussée *ground floor*
rheumatism des rhumatismes [roomah-teesm]
rib une côte [koht]
rice du riz [ree]
rich riche [reesh]
ridiculous ridicule [reedee-kool]
riding: I'd like to go riding j'aimerais faire du cheval [jaym-ray fair doo sher-val]
right: that's right c'est juste [say joost]
you're right vous avez raison [vooz ah-vay ray-zo̅n̅]
on the right à droite [ah drwaht]
a right-hand drive car une voiture avec le volant à droite [. . . voh-lo̅n̅ ah drwaht]
ring *(on finger)* une bague [bag]
ripe *(fruit)* mûr [moor]
river une rivière [reev-yair]
(main river) un fleuve [flerv]
road une route [root]
which is the road to . . .? quelle est la route pour . . .?
rob: I've been robbed on m'a dévalisé [o̅n̅ mah dayvah-lee-zay]
rock *(stone)* un rocher [roh-shay]
on the rocks avec de la glace [ah-vek der lah glahs]
roll *(bread) the closest equivalent would be:* un petit pain [per-tee pa̅n̅]
Roman Catholic catholique [kahtoh-leek]
romantic romantique [rohmo̅n̅-teek]
roof le toit [twah]
roof rack la galerie [gal-ree]
room: there isn't enough room il n'y a pas assez de place [eeln-yah pahz ah-say der plahs]
have you got a single/double room? est-ce que vous avez une chambre pour une personne/deux personnes? [. . . oon sho̅n̅br poor oon pair-son . . .]
for one night/two nights pour une nuit/deux nuits [poor oon nwee, der nwee]
YOU MAY THEN HEAR . . .
c'est complet [say ko̅n̅-play] *sorry, we're full up*

avec douche [doosh] *with shower*
avec cabinet de toilette [kahbee-nay der twah-let] *with private toilet*
avec salle de bain [sahl der b̅a̅n̅] *with private bathroom*
room number le numéro de la chambre [noomay-roh . . .]
room service le service des chambres [sair-vees . . .]
rope une corde [kord]
rose une rose [rohz]
rosé: a bottle of rosé une bouteille de rosé [boo-tay der roh-zay]
rough: the sea is rough la mer est mauvaise [lah mair ay moh-vayz]
roughly approximativement [ahproxee-mah-teev-m̅o̅n̅]
round *(circular)* rond [r̅o̅n̅]
it's my round c'est ma tournée [say mah toor-nay]
round trip un voyage aller et retour [. . . ah-lay ay rer-toor]
roundabout un rond-point [r̅o̅n̅-pw̅a̅n̅]
» *TRAVEL TIP: let cars coming from the right go first, even when you are on the roundabout*
route un itinéraire [eetee-nay-rair]
which is the prettiest/fastest route? quel est l'itinéraire le plus agréable/rapide?
» *TRAVEL TIP: route planning will be easier with the yellow Michelin road maps (1 cm = 2 km); secondary roads are generally good, and a sensible alternative to M-ways*
routiers *'relais routiers' are good inexpensive restaurants catering primarily for transport drivers; don't hesitate to try them (look for a red and blue circular sign)*
rowing boat une barque [bark]
rubber du caoutchouc [kah-oo-tshoo]
rubber band un élastique [aylass-teek]
rubbish les ordures [ohr-door]
when is rubbish collected? quand est-ce qu'il y a le ramassage des ordures [k̅o̅n̅t eskeel yah le rahmah-sahj . . .]
it's rubbish ça ne vaut rien [sahn voh ree-y̅a̅n̅]
rucksack un sac à dos [sak ah doh]
rudder le gouvernail [goovair-nah-ee]
rude impoli [a̅n̅poh-lee]

rum du rhum [rom]
run courir [koo-reer]
(engine) marcher [mahr-shay]
hurry, run! vite, dépêchez-vous! [veet daypay-shay-voo]
I've run out of petrol/money je n'ai plus d'essence/d'argent [jer nay ploo day-so̅n̅s, dahr-jo̅n̅]
he ran into my car il est rentré dans ma voiture [eel ay ro̅n̅-tray do̅n̅ . . .]
sables mouvants *quicksand*
sad triste [treest]
safe sans danger [so̅n̅ do̅n̅-jay]
will it be safe here? est-ce que ça ne risque rien ici? [. . . reesk ree-ya̅n̅ ee-see]
is it safe to swim here? est-ce qu'on peut se baigner sans danger, ici? [esko̅n̅ per ser bayn-yay so̅n̅ do̅n̅-jay . . .]
safety sécurité [saykoo-ree-tay]
safety pin épingle de sureté [ay-pa̅n̅gl der soor-tay]
sail une voile [vwahl]
can we go sailing? est-ce qu'on peut faire de la voile? [esko̅n̅ per fair . . .]
» *TRAVEL TIP: check weather conditions at the 'capitainerie' (harbour master's office)*
sailor un marin [mah-ra̅n̅]
salad une salade [sah-lad]
» *TRAVEL TIP: do not expect salad cream; salad is usually a green salad, served with a French dressing*
sale: is it for sale? est-ce qu'on peut l'acheter? [esko̅n̅ per lash-tay]
salle à manger *dining room*
salle d'attente *waiting room*
salmon le saumon [soh-mo̅n̅]
salt le sel
same le (la) même [maim]
the same again, please la même chose, s'il vous plaît [lah maim shohz . . .]
the same to you à vous pareillement [ah voo pahray-ee-mo̅n̅]
it's all the same to me ça m'est égal [sah mait ay-gal]
sample *(a wine etc)* goûter [goo-tay]
(of product) un échantillon [aysho̅n̅-tee-yo̅n̅]
sand le sable [sahbl]

sandals des sandales [sōn-dahl]
sandwich un sandwich
ham/cheese sandwich sandwich au jambon/ fromage [. . . oh jōn-bōn, froh-mahj]
» *TRAVEL TIP: not made with square sliced bread; usually a section of French stick sliced lengthways*
sanitary towel une serviette hygiénique [sairv-yet eej-yay-neek]
sans issue *no through way*
satisfactory satisfaisant [sahtees-fer-zōn]
Saturday samedi [sam-dee]
sauce la sauce [sohz]
saucepan une casserole [kas-rohl]
saucer une soucoupe [soo-koop]
sauna un sauna [soh-nah]
sausage une saucisse [soh-sees]
(cold) un saucisson [sohsee-sōn]
» *TRAVEL TIP: very different from the sausages you are used to, except for Frankfurters; a 'saucisson' (salami-type sausage) with a French loaf will make a tasty picnic*
save *(life)* sauver [soh-vay]
say: how do you say in French . . .? comment est-ce qu'on dit en français . . .? [koh-mōnt eskōn dee ōn frōn-say]
what did he say? qu'est-ce qu'il a dit? [kes-keel ah dee]
scarf un foulard [foo-lar]
scenery le paysage [payee-zahj]
schedule *(timetable)* un horaire [oh-rair]
(programme) un programme
on schedule à l'heure [ah lerr]
behind schedule en retard [rer-tahr]
scheduled flight un vol régulier [vol raygool-yay]
school une école [ay-kol]
scissors une paire de ciseaux [pair der see-zoh]
Scotland l'Ecosse [ay-kos]
Scottish écossais [aykoh-say]
scrambled eggs des oeufs brouillés [er broo-yay]
scratch une éraflure [ayrah-floor]
scream: I heard somebody scream j'ai entendu quelqu'un crier [. . . kree-yay]
screw une vis [vees]

screwdriver un tournevis [toorner-vees]
sea la mer [mair]
by the sea au bord de la mer [oh bor der . . .]
seafood des fruits de mer [frweed mair]
seafront le bord de mer [bor der mair]
search chercher [shair-shay]
search party une expédition de secours [expay-dees-yo̅n̅ der ser-koor]
seasick: I get/feel seasick j'ai le mal de mer [jay ler mal der mair]
seaside le bord de la mer [bor der lah mair]
season une saison [say-zo̅n̅]
high/low season haute/basse saison [oht, bahs . . .]
season ticket une carte d'abonnement [kart dahbon-mo̅n̅]
seasoning l'assaisonnement [ahsay-zon-mo̅n̅]
seat *(in train etc)* une place [plahs]
(chair etc) un siège [see-yayj]
is this somebody's seat? est-ce que cette place est occupée? [esker set plahs ayt ohkoo-pay]
seat belt une ceinture de sécurité [sa̅n̅-toor der saykoo-ree-tay]
» *TRAVEL TIP: wearing of seat belts compulsory outside towns*
I'd like a window seat/a seat facing the engine j'aimerais une place près de la fenêtre/dans le sens de la marche [. . . pray der lah fer-naitr, do̅n̅ ler so̅n̅s der lah marsh]
seaweed des algues [alg]
second une seconde [ser-go̅n̅d]
(2nd) deuxième [derz-yem], *(date)* le deux [der]
second hand d'occasion [dohkahz-yo̅n̅]
secretary une secrétaire [serkray-tair]
sedative un calmant [kal-mo̅n̅]
see: I see je vois [vwah]
can I see the room? est-ce que je peux voir la chambre? [. . . vwahr . . .]
have you seen . . .? est-ce que vous avez vu? [. . . voo]
see you à bientôt [ah bee-ya̅n̅-toh]
see you tonight/tomorrow à ce soir/demain [ah ser swahr, der-ma̅n̅]

seem: it seems that... il semble que... [eel sōnbl ker]
self: self-service self-service [... sair-vees]
self-contained indépendant [ānday-pōn-dōn]
sell vendre [vōndr]
send envoyer [ōnvwah-yay]
sens unique *one way*
sensitive sensible [sōn-seebl]
separate[1] séparer [saypah-ray]
I'm separated je suis séparé de ma femme [jer swee saypah-ray der mah fam]
(woman) je suis séparée de mon mari [... der mōn mah-ree]
separate[2] séparé
can we pay separately? est-ce qu'on peut payer chacun pour soi? [eskōn per pay-yay shah-kān poor swah]
September: in September en septembre [sep-tōnbr]
serious sérieux [sair-yer]
is it serious? *(injury etc)* est-ce que c'est grave? [... grahv]
serrez à droite *keep to the right*
serum *(for snake bite)* du sérum [say-rom]
serve: are you serving breakfast now? est-ce que vous servez le petit-déjeuner maintenant? [... sair-vay ...]
service le service [sair-vees]
is the service charge included? est-ce que le service est compris?
service station une station-service [stahs-yōn sair-vees]
serviette une serviette [sairv-yet]
set *(fix)* fixer [fee-xay]
(adjust) régler [ray-glay]
several plusieurs [plooz-yerr]
sew coudre [koodr]
shade: in the shade à l'ombre [ah lōnbr]
shake secouer [serkoo-ay]
» *TRAVEL TIP: shaking hands ('se serrer la main') is common on meeting and leaving somebody*
shallow peu profond [per proh-fōn]
shame: it's a shame c'est dommage [doh-mahj]
shampoo un shampooing [shōn-pwān]
shampoo and set une mise en plis [meez ōn plee]

shandy une bière panachée [bee-yair pahnah-shay]
» *TRAVEL TIP: likely to be lager and lemonade*
shape la forme [form]
share partager [pahrtah-jay]
sharp *(blade etc)* coupant [koo-pōn]
shave: I must shave je dois me raser [. . . mer rah-zay]
shaver un rasoir [rah-zwahr]
shaving foam de la mousse à raser [moos ah rah-zay]
shaving point une prise-rasoir [preez . . .]
she elle [el]
sheep un mouton [moo-tōn]
sheet un drap [drah]
(paper) une feuille de papier [fer-ee der pahp-yay]
shelf une étagère [aytah-jair]
shell *(egg, nut)* la coquille [koh-kee]
(sea) un coquillage [kohkee-yahj]
shellfish des coquillages
shelter un abri [ah-bree]
can we shelter here? est-ce que nous pouvons nous abriter ici? [. . . nooz ahbree-tay ee-see]
sherry un xérès [gzay-res]
shin le tibia [teeb-yah]
ship un bateau [bah-toh]
shirt une chemise [sher-meez]
see **chest, collar**
shock un choc [shok]
I got an electric shock from j'ai reçu une décharge électrique de [jay rer-soo oon day-sharj aylek-treek]
shock-absorber un amortisseur [ahmor-tee-serr]
shoes des chaussures [shoh-soor]
» *TRAVEL TIP: shoe sizes*

UK	*4*	*5*	*6*	*7*	*8*	*9*	*10*	*11*
Continent	*37*	*38*	*39*	*41*	*42*	*43*	*44*	*46*

shop un magasin [mahgah-zān]
shopping: I've got some shopping to do j'ai des courses à faire [jay day koors ah fair]
» *TRAVEL TIP: opening hours: food shops usually 7.30 to 12.30 and 15.30 to 19.30; other shops 9 to 12 and 14 to 19; closing day gen. Mon (or half day Mon); bakers and small grocers often open on Sun morning*
shore: on the shore sur le rivage [. . . ree-vahj]
short court [koor]
I'm 3 short il m'en manque trois [eel mōn mōnk . . .]

short cut un raccourci [rahkoor-see]
shorts un short
shoulder l'épaule [ay-pohl]
shout crier [kree-yay]
show *(exhibition)* une exposition [expoh-zees-yon̄]
(theatre etc) un spectacle [spek-tahkl]
please show me montrez-moi, s'il vous plaît [mon̄-tray mwah . . .]
shower une douche [doosh]
shrimps des crevettes grises [krer-vet greez]
shrink: does it shrink? est-ce que ça rétrécit? [esker sah raytray-see]
shut fermer [fair-may]
when do you shut? vous fermez à quelle heure? [voo fair-may ah kel err]
shut up! taisez-vous! [tay-zay-voo]
shy timide [tee-meed]
sick malade [mah-lad]
I feel sick je ne me sens pas bien [jer ner mer son̄ pah bee-yan̄]
he's been sick il a vomi [eel ah voh-mee]
side le côté
on this side de ce côté
on the other side de l'autre côté
side lights les feux de position [fer der pohzees-yon̄]
side street une rue de traverse [roo der trah-vairs]
by the side of the road au bord de la route [oh bor der lah root]
sight: out of sight hors de vue [or der voo]
the sights of . . . les choses à voir dans . . . [lay shohz ah vwahr . . .]
we'd like to go on a sightseeing tour nous voudrions faire une visite guidée [noo voodree-yon̄ fair oon vee-zet ghee-day]
sign *(road)* un panneau [pah-noh]
(notice) un écriteau [aykree-toh]
signal: he didn't signal il n'a pas mis son clignotant [. . . mee son̄ kleen-yoh-ton̄]
signature une signature [seen-yah-toor]
silencer le silencieux [seelon̄s-yer]
silk la soie [swah]
silly stupide [stoo-peed]

silver: a silver chain une chaînette en argent [. . . o̅n̅n ahr-jo̅n̅]
similar semblable [so̅n̅-blahbl]
simple simple [sa̅n̅pl]
since: since last week depuis la semaine dernière [der-pwee . . .]
  since we arrived depuis notre arrivée
  since you want . . . puisque vous voulez . . . [pwees-ker . . .]
sincerely *see* **letter**
sing chanter [sho̅n̅-tay]
single: single room une chambre pour une personne [sho̅n̅br poor oon pair-son]
  I'm single je suis célibataire [jer swee saylee-bah-tair]
  I'd like a single to j'aimerais un billet aller pour [. . . bee-yay ah-lay . . .]
sink *(boat)* couler [koo-lay]
  (kitchen) l'évier [ayv-yay]
Sir . . . Monsieur . . . [mers-yer]
  see **letter**
sister: my sister ma soeur [serr]
sit: can I sit here est-ce que je peux m'asseoir ici [. . . ah-swahr . . .]
  sit next to me asseyez-vous à côté de moi [ahsay-yay voo . . .]
size la taille [tie]
  (of shoes) la pointure [pwa̅n̅-toor]
  do you have my size? est-ce que vous avez ma taille/pointure? [esker vooz ah-vay . . .]
  YOU MAY HEAR OR SEE . . .
  petit [per-tee] *small*
  moyen [mwah-ya̅n̅] *medium*
  grand [gro̅n̅] *large*
skates des patins [pah-ta̅n̅]
  skating rink une patinoire [pahtee-nwahr]
skis des skis [skee]
  skiing boots des chaussures de ski [shoh-soor . . .]
  ski poles des bâtons de ski [bah-to̅n̅ . . .]
  ski lift un remonte-pente [rer-mo̅n̅t-po̅n̅t]
  ski run une piste [peest]
skid déraper [dayrah-pay]
skin la peau [poh]

skin-diving la plongée sous-marine [plon̄-jay soo-mah-reen]
skirt une jupe [joop]
sky le ciel [see-yel]
sledge une luge [looj]
sleep: I can't sleep je ne peux pas dormir [. . . dor-meer]
sleeper *(train)* un wagon-lit [vah-gon̄-lee]
sleeping bag un sac de couchage [sak der koo-shahj]
sleeping pills des somnifères [somnee-fair]
sleeve une manche [mon̄sh]
slice une tranche [tron̄sh]
slides *(photo)* des diapositives [dee-yah-poh-zee-teev]
slippery glissant [glee-son̄]
slow lent [lon̄]
could you speak a little slower? est-ce que vous pouvez parler un peu plus lentement? [. . . an̄ per ploo lon̄t-mon̄]
small petit [per-tee]
small change de la petite monnaie [per-teet moh-nay]
smallpox la variole [vahr-yohl]
smell: there's a funny smell il y a une odeur bizarre [eelyah oon oh-derr . . .]
it smells ça sent [sah son̄]
smoke la fumée [foo-may]
do you smoke? est-ce que vous fumez? [esker voo foo-may]
can I smoke? est-ce que je peux fumer?
» *TRAVEL TIP: smoking is prohibited in France in public buildings and on public transport, as well as in cinemas*
snack un casse-croûte [kahs-kroot]
snake un serpent [sair-pon̄]
S.N.C.F. *the French Railways*
snorkel un tuba [too-bah]
snow la neige [nej]
powder snow la neige poudreuse [. . . poo-drerz]
so: it's so hot that. . . il fait si chaud que . . . [eel fay see shoh ker]
not so much pas tant [pah-ton̄]
so so comme çi, comme ça [komsee-komsah]
soaked: we are soaked nous sommes trempés [noo som tron̄-pay]

soap un savon [sah-vo̅n̅]
soap powder *(washing)* du détergent [daytair-jo̅n̅]
socks une paire de chaussettes [pair der shoh-set]
soda water de l'eau [oh] de seltz
soft doux [doo]
soft drinks des boissons sans alcool [bwah-so̅n̅ so̅n̅z al-kol]
soldes *sale*
sole *(fish)* une sole
(shoe) une semelle [ser-mel]
could you put new soles on these? est-ce que vous pouvez ressemeler ces chaussures? [. . . rers-mer-lay say shoh-soor]
some: some places certains endroits [sair-ta̅n̅ . . .]
can I have some? est-ce que je peux en avoir? [esker jer per o̅n̅n ah-vwahr]
some bread du [doo] pain; **some beer** de la [der lah] bière; **some crisps** des [day] chips
can I have some more? est-ce que je peux en avoir plus? [. . . o̅n̅n ah-vwahr ploos]
somebody quelqu'un [kel-ka̅n̅]
something quelque chose [kel-ker shohz]
sometimes quelquefois [kelker-fwah]
somewhere quelque part [kel-ker par]
son: my son mon fils [fees]
song une chanson [sho̅n̅-so̅n̅]
sonnez *please ring*
soon bientôt [bee-ya̅n̅-toh]
as soon as possible dès que possible [day ker poh-seebl]
sooner plus tôt [ploo toh]
sore: it's sore ça fait mal [sah fay mal]
I have a sore throat j'ai mal à la gorge [jay mal ah lah gohrj]
sorry: I'm sorry excusez-moi [exkoo-zay-mwah]
sort: what sort of? quelle sorte de? [kel sort der]
will you sort the problem out? est-ce que vous pouvez arranger ça? [. . . ahro̅n̅-jay sah]
sortie de camions *lorries crossing*
sortie de secours *emergency exit*
sound: it sounds interesting ça a l'air intéressant [sah ah lair . . .]
soup une soupe [soop]

sour aigre [aigr]
sous-sol *basement*
south le sud [sood]
South Africa l'Afrique du Sud [ah-freek . . .]
souvenir un souvenir [soov-neer]
spade *(for beach)* une pelle [pel]
Spain l'Espagne [es-pan]
in Spain en Espagne [onn . . .]
Spanish espagnol [espan-yol]
spanner une clé anglaise [klay on-glayz]
spare: spare parts des pièces de rechange [pee-yes der rer-shonj]
spare wheel la roue de secours [roo der ser-koor]
sparking plugs les bougies [boo-jee]
speak: do you speak English? est-ce que vous parlez anglais? [esker voo par-lay on-glay]
is there somebody who speaks English? est-ce qu'il y a quelqu'un qui parle anglais? [. . . kel-kan kee parl on-glay]
I don't speak French je ne parle pas français [jer ner parl pah fron-say]
special spécial [spays-yal]
specialist un spécialiste [spays-yah-leest]
specially spécialement [spays-yal-mon]
spectacles des lunettes [loo-net]
speed la vitesse [vee-tes]
he was speeding il allait trop vite [eel ah-lay troh veet]
speed limit une limitation de vitesse [leemee-tahs-yon . . .]
speedometer le compteur de vitesse [kon-terr]
» *TRAVEL TIP: speed limit: in towns 60 km/h (38 mph); on roads 90 km/h (56 mph); on dual carriageways 110 km/h (70 mph); on M-ways 130 km/h (81 mph)*
spell: how do you spell it? comment ça s'écrit? [koh-mon sah say-kree]
spend *(money)* dépenser
(time) passer
spices des condiments [kondee-mon]
is it spicy? est-ce que c'est très épicé? [. . . aypee-say]
spider une araignée [ahrain-yay]
spirits des spiritueux [spee-ree-too-er]
spoon une cuillère [kwee-yair]

sprain une entorse [on-tohrs]
I've sprained my ankle je me suis foulé la cheville [jer mer swee foo-lay . . .]
spring *(season)* le printemps [pran-ton]
(metal) un ressort [rer-sor]
(water) une source [soors]
square *(in town)* une place [plahs]
2 square metres deux mètres carrés [. . . maitr kah-ray]
staff le personnel [pairsoh-nel]
stairs les escaliers [eskahl-yay]
stalls: 2 stalls deux orchestre [derz or-kestr]
stamp: 2 stamps for Great Britain deux timbres [tanbr] pour la Grande-Bretagne
» *TRAVEL TIP: you can buy stamps from many newsagents and some cafés; look for the sign 'tabacs-journaux' or 'tabac'*
stand *(at fair)* un stand [ston]
standard normal
star une étoile [ay-twahl]
starboard: to starboard à tribord [ah tree-bor]
start commencer [kohmon-say]
my car won't start ma voiture ne démarre pas [mah vwah-toor ner day-mar pah]
when does it start? ça commence quand? [sah koh-mons kon]
starter *(car)* le démarreur [daymah-rerr]
(dish) une entrée [on-tray]
starving: I'm starving je meurs de faim [jer merr der fan]
station la gare [gar]
(underground) la station de métro [stahs-yon . . .]
stationer's une papeterie [pahpet-ree]
stationnement *parking*
statue une statue [stah-too]
stay: we enjoyed our stay nous avons fait un très bon séjour [. . . say-joor]
stay there restez là [res-tay lah]
I'm staying at . . . je séjourne à . . . [say-joorn]
steak un steak [stek]
YOU MAY HEAR . . .
à point [ah pwan] *medium*
bien cuit [bee-yan kwee] *well done*

saignant [sayn-yōn] *rare*
steal voler [voh-lay]
steep *(slope)* raide [red]
steering *(car)* la direction [deereks-yōn]
steering wheel le volant [voh-lōn]
step *(stairs)* une marche [marsh]
stereo stéréo [stay-ray-oh]
sterling: in sterling en livres sterling [ōn leevr stair-ling]
stewardess une hôtesse [oh-tes]
sticking plaster un pansement adhésif [pōns-mōn ahday-zeef]
sticky poisseux [pwah-ser]
stiff dur [door]
still: keep still restez tranquille [res-tay trōn-keel]
I'm still here je suis encore là [jer swee ōn-kor . . .]
stockings des bas [bah]
stolen: my wallet's been stolen on m'a volé mon portefeuille [ōn mah voh-lay . . .]
stomach l'estomac [estoh-mah]
I've got a stomach-ache j'ai mal au ventre [jay mal oh vōntr]
have you got something for an upset stomach? est-ce que vous avez quelque chose pour les maux de ventre? [. . . moh der vōntr]
stone une pierre [pee-yair]
» *TRAVEL TIP: weight: 1 stone = 6.35 kg*
stop s'arrêter [. . . ahray-tay]
do you stop near . . .? est-ce que vous vous arrêtez près de . . .? [esker voo vooz ahray-tay pray der]
stop over une escale [es-kahl]
storm une tempête [tōn-pet]
straight droit [drwah]
(whisky etc) sec
go straight on continuez tout droit [kōntee-noo-ay too drwah]
straight away immédiatement [eemayd-yat-mōn]
strange bizarre
stranger un inconnu [ānkoh-noo]
I'm a stranger here je ne suis pas d'ici [jer ner swee pah dee-see]
strap une courroie [koo-rwah]
strawberries des fraises [frayz]

street une rue [roo]
  a street map of un plan de [plo̅n̅]
strike une grève [graiv]
string de la ficelle [fee-sel]
stroke: he's had a stroke il a eu une attaque [. . . ah-tak]
strong fort [for]
stuck coincé [kwa̅n̅-say]
student un étudiant [aytood-yo̅n̅]
stung: I've been stung by . . . j'ai été piqué par . . . [jay ay-tay pee-kay par]
stupid stupide [stoo-peed]
suburbs la banlieue [bo̅n̅l-yer]
successful: was it successful? est-ce que ça a réussi? [esker sah ah ray-oo-see]
such: such a lot of . . . tant de . . . [to̅n̅ der]
suddenly subitement [soobeet-mo̅n̅]
suffer: he's suffering from il souffre de [soofr der]
sugar du sucre [sookr]
» *TRAVEL TIP: sugar in lumps is the rule; if you want granulated sugar, ask for 'du sucre en poudre'* [sookr o̅n̅ poodr]
suit *(man's)* un complet [ko̅n̅-play]
  (woman's) un tailleur [tah-yerr]
suitable: it's not suitable ça ne convient pas [sah ner ko̅n̅v-ya̅n̅ pah]
suitcase une valise [vah-leez]
summer l'été [ay-tay]
sun le soleil [soh-lay]
  in the sun au soleil
  out of the sun à l'abri du soleil [ah lah-bree . . .]
  sunbathe se bronzer [ser bro̅n̅-zay]
  sunburn un coup de soleil [koo . . .]
  sunglasses des lunettes de soleil [loo-net . . .]
  sunstroke une insolation [a̅n̅soh-lahs-yo̅n̅]
  suntan oil de l'huile solaire [weel soh-lair]
Sunday dimanche [dee-mo̅n̅sh]
supermarket un supermarché [soopair-mar-shay]
» *TRAVEL TIP: often open on Sun mornings*
supper le souper [soo-pay]
» *TRAVEL TIP: supper is not served, as lunch is a main meal and dinner is served around 7 or 8 pm*
sure: I'm not sure je ne suis pas sûr [. . . soor]

sure! bien entendu! [bee-yann onton-doo]
are you sure? vous êtes sûr? [vooz ayt soor]
surfboard une planche de surf [plonsh der soorf]
surfing: to go surfing faire du surf [fair du soorf]
surname le nom de famille [non der fah-mee]
sweat transpirer [tronspee-ray]
sweater un pull [pool]
sweet *(dessert)* un dessert [day-sair]
it's too sweet c'est trop sucré [. . . soo-kray]
swerve: I had to swerve j'ai dû donner un coup de volant [jay doo doh-nay an koo der voh-lon]
swim: I can't swim je ne sais pas nager [jer ner say pah nah-jay]
I'm going for a swim je vais me baigner [jer vay mer bayn-yay]
swimming costume un maillot de bain [mah-yoh der ban]
swimming trunks un slip de bain
swimming pool une piscine [pee-seen]
switch un interrupteur [antay-roop-terr]
switch the light on/off allumez/éteignez la lumière [ahloo-may, aytayn-yay . . .]
switchboard le standard [ston-dar]
Swiss suisse [swees]
Switzerland la Suisse [swees]
tabac-journaux *tobacconist and newsagent*
table: a table for 4 une table pour quatre [oon tahbl poor kahtr]
table wine du vin ordinaire [van ohrdee-nair]
taille *size*
take prendre [prondr]
can I take this with me? est-ce que je peux emporter ça? [. . . onpohr-tay . . .]
take me to the airport emmenez-moi à l'aéroport [onm-nay mwah . . .]
can I take you out tonight? est-ce que vous voulez sortir avec moi ce soir? [. . . sohr-teer ah-vek mwah ser swahr]
is this seat taken? est-ce que cette place est prise? [. . . set plahs ay preez]
talcum powder du talc
talk parler [par-lay]
tall grand [gron]

tampons des tampons hygiéniques [tonpon eej-yay-neek]
tan le bronzage [bron-zahj]
I want to get a tan je veux bronzer [jer ver bron-zay]
tank le réservoir [rayzair-vwahr]
tap le robinet [rohbee-nay]
tape une bande magnétique [bond mahn-yay-teek]
tape-recorder un magnétophone [mahn-yay-toh-fon]
tariff le tarif [tah-reef]
taste: what does it taste like? quel goût ça a? [kel goo sah ah]
can I taste it? est-ce que je peux goûter? [esker jer per goo-tay]
it tastes horrible/very nice c'est affreux/délicieux [sayt ah-frer, daylees-yer]
taxi un taxi [tah-xee]
will you get me a taxi? est-ce que vous pouvez m'appeler un taxi? [. . . map-lay an tah-xee]
where can I get a taxi? où est-ce que je peux trouver un taxi?
stop here arrêtez-vous ici [ahray-tay-voo ee-see]
YOU MAY SEE . . .
tête de station *taxi stance*
» *TRAVEL TIP: don't forget to tip (about 10%)*
T.C.F. *= Touring Club de France, similar to AA or RAC*
tea le thé [tay]
could I have a cup of tea? est-ce que je peux avoir un thé?
a pot of tea for 2 une théière pour deux [tay-yair poor der]
YOU MAY THEN HEAR . . .
un thé lait [tay lay] *tea with milk*
un thé citron [tay see-tron] *lemon tea*
» *TRAVEL TIP: tea is not automatically served with milk*
teach: could you teach me French? est-ce que vous pouvez m'apprendre le français? [. . . mah-prondr ler fron-say]
teacher le professeur [prohfay-serr]
teinturerie *dry cleaner's*
telegram: I want to send a telegram je veux envoyer un télégramme [. . . onvwah-yay an taylay-gram]
telephone le téléphone [taylay-fon]
(where) can I make a phone-call? (où) est-ce que je

peux téléphoner? [. . . taylay-foh-nay]
can I speak to . . .? est-ce que je peux parler à . . .? [esker jer per pahr-lay ah]
could you get this number for me? est-ce que vous pouvez m'appeler ce numéro? [. . . map-lay ser noomay-roh]
extension . . . poste numéro . . . [pohst noomay-roh]
telephone directory l'annuaire du téléphone [ahnoo-air . . .]
YOU MAY HEAR . . .
qui est à l'appareil? *who's speaking?*
c'est un faux numéro *sorry wrong number*
la ligne est occupée *the line is engaged*
ça ne répond pas *there is no answer*
ne quittez pas, je vous passe . . . *hold the line, I'm putting you through to . . .*
» *TRAVEL TIP: you can phone from most cafés: pay at counter or you may have to buy a 'jeton'* [jer-ton] *(token) which you insert in the pay phone; there are now more call boxes, esp. in Paris (grey colour): insert coin (50 centimes for local call) before lifting receiver; if you get somebody to call you back from the UK: 010 33 plus town prefix without the 0; see numbers on last page*
television: I'd like to watch television j'aimerais regarder la télévision [jaim-ray rergahr-day lah taylay-veez-yon]
tell: could you tell me where/if . . .? est-ce que vous pouvez me dire où/si . . .? [esker voo poo-vay mer deer oo, see]
temperature la température [tonpay-rah-toor]
he's got a temperature il a de la température
temporary provisoire [prohvee-zwahr]
tennis: do you play tennis? est-ce que vous jouez au tennis? [. . . joo-ay oh tay-nees]
tennis court un court de tennis [koor . . .]
tennis racquet une raquette de tennis [rah-ket . . .]
tennis ball une balle de tennis [bahl . . .]
tent une tente [tont]
terminus le terminus [tairmee-noos]
terrible terrible [tay-reebl]
(bad) affreux [ah-frer]
terrific fantastique [fontahs-teek]
than: bigger than . . . plus grand que . . . [. . . ker]

thanks merci [mair-see]; **no thanks** non merci
thank you very much merci beaucoup [. . . boh-koo]
thank you for your help merci de votre aide
that ce (cette) [ser, set]
that man/plane cet homme/avion [set . . .]
I would like that one j'aimerais celui-là (celle-là) [. . . serlwee-lah, sel-lah]
and that? et ça? [. . . sah]
I think that . . . je crois que . . . [. . . ker]
the le (la), les [ler, lah, lay]
the children les enfants [layz . . .]
the airport l'aéroport
theatre le théâtre [tay-ahtr]
their leur, leurs [lerr]
their car leur voiture, **their children** leurs enfants
it's their suitcase, it's theirs c'est leur valise, c'est la leur
them: with them avec eux (elles) [. . . er, el]
we didn't see them nous ne les avons pas vus [. . . lay . . .]
we gave them the money nous leur avons donné l'argent [. . . lerr . . .]
then ensuite [on-sweet]
there là [lah]
how do I get there? comment est-ce qu'on y va? [koh-mon eskonn ee vah]
there is, there are il y a [eel-yah]
there isn't, there aren't il n'y a pas de [eeln-yah pah der]
is there a bus? est-ce qu'il y a un bus? [eskeel-yah . . .]
there you are *(giving something)* voilà [vwah-lah]
these: these apples ces pommes [say . . .]
can I take these? est-ce que je peux prendre ceux-ci (celles-ci)? [. . . ser-see, sel-see]
they ils (elles) [eel, el]
thick épais [ay-pay]
thief un voleur [voh-ler]
thigh la cuisse [kwees]
thin mince [mans]
thing une chose [shohz]
I've lost all my things j'ai perdu toutes mes affaires [jay pair-doo toot mayz ah-fair]

think: I'll think it over je vais y réfléchir [jer vayz ee rayflay-sheer]
I think so je crois [jer krwah]
I don't think so je ne crois pas
I think that . . . je crois que . . .
third troisième [trwahz-yem]
thirsty: I'm thirsty j'ai soif [jay swahf]
this ce (cette) [ser, set]
this man/plane cet homme/avion [set . . .]
I would like this one j'aimerais celui-ci (celle-ci) [serlwee-see, sel-see]
this is my wife/Mr . . . voici ma femme/Monsieur . . . [vwah-see . . .]
this is . . . c'est . . . [say]
is this . . .? est-ce que c'est . . .? [esker say]
and this? et ça? [. . . sah]
those: those people ces gens [say jon]
how much are those? combien coûtent ceux-ci (celles-ci)? [. . . ser-see, sel-see]
thread du fil [feel]
three trois [trwah]
throat la gorge [gorj]
throat lozenges des pastilles pour la gorge [pas-tee . . .]
through à travers [ah trah-vair]
throw lancer [lon-say]
thumb le pouce [poos]
thunder le tonnerre [toh-nair]
thunderstorm un orage [oh-rahj]
Thursday jeudi [jer-dee]
ticket un billet [bee-yay]
tie *(necktie)* une cravate [krah-vat]
tight *(clothes)*: **they're too tight** ils sont trop justes [. . . joost]
tights des collants [koh-lon]
time: what's the time? quelle heure il est? [kayl err eel ay]
at what time? à quelle heure?
I haven't got time je n'ai pas le temps [. . . ler ton]
for the time being pour le moment [. . . moh-mon]
this time cette fois [set fwah]
last/next time la dernière/prochaine fois [dairn-yair, proh-shain fwah]

3 times trois fois
have a good time! amusez-vous bien! [ahmoo-zay-voo bee-yañ]
HOW TO TELL THE TIME:
it's 2 am/pm c'est deux heures du matin/de l'après-midi [say derz err doo mahtañ, der lah-pray-mee-dee]
at 7 pm à sept heures du soir [ah set err doo swahr]
2.05 deux heures cinq
2.15 deux heures et quart [. . . ay kar]
2.30 deux heures et demie [. . . ay der-mee]
2.40 trois heures moins vingt [. . . mwañ vañ]
2.45 trois heures moins le quart [. . . mwañ ler kar]
timetable un horaire [oh-rair]
tin une boîte [bwaht]
tin-opener un ouvre-boîte [oovrer-bwaht]
tip: is the tip included? est-ce que le pourboire est compris? [. . . poor-bwahr . . .]
» *TRAVEL TIP: tip usherettes (about 2F), taxi drivers, and lavatory attendants (about 50 centimes)*
tired: I'm tired je suis fatigué [fahtee-gay]
tirez *pull*
tissues des Kleenex
to: to Paris à Paris
to our friends' chez [shay] nos amis
to England/Scotland en [oñ] Angleterre/Ecosse
toast un toast [tohst]
tobacco du tabac [tah-bah]
tobacconist's un bureau de tabac [boo-roh der tah-bah]
today aujourd'hui [ohjoor-dwee]
toe le doigt de pied [dwah der pee-yay]
together: we're together nous sommes ensemble [. . . oñ-soñbl]
toilet: where are the toilets? où sont les toilettes? [oo soñ lay twah-let]
I have to go to the toilet je dois aller aux toilettes [jer dwahz ah-lay oh . . .]
there's no toilet paper il n'y a pas de papier hygiénique [. . . pahp-yay eej-yay-neek]
tomato une tomate [toh-mat]
tomato juice un jus [joo] de tomate
tomato ketchup *you will not find tomato ketchup ('le ketchup'* [ket-sherp]*) in a French restaurant, unless it's a fast food establishment*

tomorrow demain [der-mān̄]
tomorrow morning/afternoon/evening demain matin/après-midi/soir [der-mān̄ mah-tān̄, ahpray-mee-dee, swahr]
the day after tomorrow après-demain [ahpray-der-mān̄]
ton une tonne [ton]
» *TRAVEL TIP: 1 ton = 1,016 kilos*
tongue la langue [lōn̄g]
tonic *(water)* un schweppes [shveps]
tonight ce soir [ser swahr]
tonne une tonne [ton]
» *TRAVEL TIP: 1 tonne = 1,000 kg = metric ton*
tonsils les amygdales [ahmee-dahl]
tonsillitis une angine [ōn̄-jeen]
too trop [troh]
that's too much c'est trop
too much . . ., too many . . . trop de . . .
tool un outil [oo-tee]
tooth une dent [dōn̄]
I've got toothache j'ai mal aux dents [jay mal oh dōn̄]
toothbrush une brosse à dents [brohs ah dōn̄]
toothpaste du dentifrice [dōn̄tee-frees]
top: on top of sur [soor]
on the top floor au dernier étage [oh dairn-yair ay-tahj]
at the top en haut [ōn̄ oh]
total le total [toh-tal]
tough dur [door]
tour une excursion [exkoors-yōn̄]
we'd like to go on a tour of . . . nous aimerions visiter . . . [noozaymer-yōn̄ veezee-tay]
we're touring around nous visitons la région [noo veezee-tōn̄ lah rayj-yōn̄]
tourist: I'm a tourist je suis un touriste [. . . too-reest]
tourist office le syndicat d'initiative [sān̄dee-kah deenees-yah-teev]
toutes directions *through traffic*
tow: can you give me a tow? est-ce que vous pouvez me remorquer? [. . . mer rermohr-kay]
towrope une corde de dépannage [kord der daypah-nahj]

towards: he was coming straight towards me il venait droit vers moi [. . . drwah vair mwah]
towel une serviette [sairv-yet]
town une ville [veel]
in town en ville
would you take me into the town? est-ce que vous pouvez m'emmener en ville?
traditional traditionnel [trahdees-yoh-nel]
traffic la circulation [seerkoo-lahs-yon̄]
traffic lights les feux [fer]
traffic policeman un agent de la circulation [ah-jon̄ . . .]
train un train [tran̄]
» *TRAVEL TIP: you may have to punch your ticket before boarding the train: look for orange-coloured machines located on platforms or for the notice 'compostez votre billet'; children under 10 pay half-fare, go free under 4; there are extra charges on some inter-city trains*
traiteur *delicatessen, caterers*
tranquillizers des tranquillisants [tron̄kee-lee-zon̄]
translate: would you translate that for me? est-ce que vous pouvez me traduire ça? [. . . mer trah-dweer sah]
transmission *(of car)* la transmission [tron̄smees-yon̄]
travaux *roadworks*
travel agent's une agence de voyage [ah-jon̄s der voh-yahj]
traveller's cheque un traveller's cheque
tree un arbre [ahrbr]
trip un voyage [voh-yahj]
(short tour, drive) une excursion [exkoors-yon̄]
we want to go on a trip to . . . nous voulons faire une excursion à . . .
trouble: I'm having trouble with . . . j'ai des ennuis avec . . . [jay dayz on̄n-wee ah-vek]
trousers un pantalon [pon̄tah-lon̄]
true vrai [vray]
trunks *(swimming)* un slip de bain [. . . der ban̄]
try essayer [essay-yay]
can I try it on? est-ce que je peux l'essayer?
T-shirt un T-shirt
t.t.c. *= toutes taxes comprises (inclusive of any duties)*
Tuesday mardi [mahr-dee]

tunnel un tunnel [too-nel]
turn: where do we turn off? où est-ce qu'il faut tourner? [wes-keel foh toor-nay]
he turned without indicating il a tourné sans mettre le clignotant [. . . ler kleen-yoh-ton]
T.V.A. [tay-vay-ah] *VAT*
twice deux fois [der fwah]
twin beds des lits jumeaux [lee joo-moh]
twin room une chambre à deux lits [shonbr ah der lee]
two deux [der]
typewriter une machine à écrire [mah-sheen ah ay-kreer]
typical typique [tee-peek]
tyre un pneu [pner]
I need a new tyre il me faut un pneu neuf [eel mer foh an pner nerf]
» *TRAVEL TIP: tyre pressures*

lb/sq in	*18*	*20*	*22*	*24*	*26*	*28*	*30*
kg/sq cm	*1.3*	*1.4*	*1.5*	*1.7*	*1.8*	*2*	*2.1*

ugly laid [lay]
ulcer un ulcère [ool-sair]
(in mouth) un aphte [ahft]
umbrella un parapluie [pahrah-plwee]
uncle: my uncle mon oncle [onkl]
uncomfortable inconfortable [ankon-for-tahbl]
unconscious: he is unconscious il a perdu connaissance [eel ah pair-doo kohnay-sons]
under sous [soo]
he's under 12 il a moins de douze ans [eel ah mwan der . . .]
underdone pas assez cuit [pahz ah-say kwee]
underexposed sous-exposé [soozex-poh-zay]
underground *(rail)* le métro [may-troh]
see ***métro***
understand: I don't understand je ne comprends pas [jer ner kon-pron pah]
do you understand? est-ce que vous comprenez? [. . . konprer-nay]
undo défaire [day-fair]
United States les Etats-Unis [aytahz-oo-nee]
university l'université [oonee-vair-see-tay]
unlock ouvrir [oo-vreer]

until jusqu'à [joos-kah]
  until July jusqu'en juillet [joos-kon . . .]
unusual inhabituel [eenah-bee-too-el]
up en haut [on oh]
  he's not up yet il n'est pas encore levé [eel nay pahz on-kor ler-vay]
upside down à l'envers [ah lon-vair]
upstairs en haut [on oh]
urgent urgent [oor-jon]
us nous [noo]
USA les USA [oo-es-ah]
use: can I use . . .? est-ce que je peux utiliser . . .? [esker jer per ootee-lee-zay]
useful utile [oo-teel]
usual habituel [ahbee-too-el]
  as usual comme d'habitude [kom dahbee-tood]
  usually d'habitude [dahbee-tood]
U-turn un demi-tour [der-mee-toor]
vacancy: do you have any vacancies? est-ce que vous avez de la place? [. . . der lah plahs]
vacate *(room)* libérer [leebay-ray]
vaccination un vaccin [vak-san]
vacuum flask un thermos [tair-mohs]
valid: how long is it valid for? c'est valable combien de temps? [say vah-lahbl konb-yan der ton]
valley une vallée [vah-lay]
valuable: it's valuable ça a de la valeur [. . . vah-lerr]
  will you look after my valuables? est-ce que vous pouvez me garder mes objets de valeur? [. . . mer gahr-day mayz ob-jay der vah-lerr]
value la valeur [vah-lerr]
valves *(of car)* les soupapes [soo-pap]
van une camionnette [kahm-yoh-net]
vanilla *(ice-cream)* à la vanille [ah lah vah-nee]
varicose veins des varices [vah-rees]
veal du veau [voh]
vegetables des légumes [lay-goom]
vegetarian végétarien [vayjay-tahr-yan]
vendre: à vendre *for sale*
ventilator un ventilateur [vontee-lah-terr]
very très [tray]
  very much beaucoup [boh-koo]
view la vue [voo]

via par
village un village [vee-lahj]
vine une vigne [veen]
vinegar du vinaigre [vee-naigr]
vineyard un vignoble [veen-yohbl]
vintage: a good vintage une bonne année [bon ah-nay]
violent violent [vee-yoh-lon]
virages *bends*
visibility la visibilité [veezee-bee-lee-tay]
visit visiter [veezee-tay]
visitor une visite [vee-zeet]
vitesse limitée à . . . *speed limit . . .*
voice la voix [vwah]
voie 6 *platform 6 ('voie' is the actual track, but corresponds to the British system of platform numbering)*
voltage le voltage [vol-tahj]
is it 220V? est-ce que c'est du deux cent vingt volts? [. . . doo der son van vohlt]
waist la taille [tie]
» *TRAVEL TIP: waist measurements*

UK	*24*	*26*	*28*	*30*	*32*	*34*	*36*	*38*
Continent	*61*	*66*	*71*	*76*	*80*	*87*	*91*	*97*

wait: will we have to wait long? est-ce qu'il faudra attendre longtemps? [eskeel foh-drah ah-tondr lon-ton]
wait for me! attendez-moi! [ahton-day-mwah]
I'm waiting for j'attends [jah-ton]
waiter le serveur [sair-verr]
waiter! s'il vous plaît! [seel voo play]
waitress la serveuse [sair-verz]
waitress! s'il vous plaît! [seel-voo play]
wake: will you wake me up at 7.30? est-ce que vous pouvez me réveiller à 7.30? [. . . mer rayvay-yay . . .]
Wales le Pays de Galles [payee der gal]
walk: can we walk there? est-ce qu'on peut y aller à pied? [. . . ee ah-lay ah pee-yay]
are there any good walks around here? est-ce qu'il y a des promenades intéressantes dans les environs? [. . . day prohm-nad antay-ray-sont . . .]
walking shoes des chaussures de marche [shoh-soor der marsh]

walking stick une canne [kan]
wall le mur [moor]
wallet un portefeuille [pohrter-fer-ee]
want: I want . . . je voudrais . . . [jer voo-dray]
I want to talk to . . . je voudrais parler à . . . *(note that you can say 'je veux', but 'je voudrais' is more courteous)*
we want . . . nous voulons . . . [noo voo-l̅o̅n̅]
he wants . . . il veut . . . [eel ver]
what do you want? qu'est-ce que vous voulez? [kesker voo voo-lay]
I don't want . . . je ne veux pas . . . [jer ner ver pah]
war la guerre [gair]
warm chaud [shoh]
warn avertir [ahvair-teer]
wash: can you wash these for me? est-ce que vous pouvez me laver ça? [. . . mer lah-vay sah]
where can I wash? où est-ce que je peux me laver? [wesker jer per mer lah-vay]
washable lavable [lah-vahbl]
washbasin un lavabo [lahvah-boh]
washing powder de la poudre à lessive [poodr ah lay-seev]
washing up liquid du détergent pour la vaisselle [daytair-j̅o̅n̅ poor lah vay-sel]
washer *(for tap etc)* un joint [jw̅a̅n̅]
wasp une guêpe [gaip]
watch *(wrist-)* une montre [m̅o̅n̅tr]
my watch is slow/fast ma montre retarde/avance [. . . rer-tahrd, ah-v̅o̅n̅s]
will you watch my bags for me? est-ce que vous pouvez surveiller mes bagages? [. . . soor-vay-yay may bah-gahj]
watch out! attention! [aht̅o̅n̅s-yon]
watch strap un bracelet de montre [brahs-lay]
water l'eau [oh]
can I have some water? est-ce que je peux avoir de l'eau?
hot and cold running water eau courante chaude et froide [oh koo-r̅o̅n̅t shohd ay frwad]
waterproof imperméable [a̅n̅pair-may-ahbl]
waterskiing le ski nautique [skee noh-teek]
way: the French way à la française [ah lah fr̅o̅n̅-sayz]

could you tell me the way to . . .? quel est le chemin pour aller à . . .? [kel ay ler sher-mān poor ah-lay ah]
YOU MAY THEN HEAR . . .
tournez . . ., prenez . . . *turn . . ., go . . .*
à droite *right,* à gauche *left*
continuez tout droit *keep straight on*
aux feux *at the lights*
we nous [noo]
weak faible [faibl]
weather le temps [tōn]
what's the weather like in . . .? quel temps est-ce qu'il fait à . . .? [kel tōn eskeel fay ah]
what's the weather forecast? quelles sont les prévisions de la météo [. . . lay prayveez-yōn der lah maytay-oh]
YOU MAY THEN HEAR . . .
couvert *overcast,* du soleil *sunny,* de la neige *snow,* de la pluie *rain,* du vent *wind,* (très) froid *(very) cold,* (très) chaud *(very) warm*
wedding un mariage [mahr-yahj]
Wednesday mercredi [mairkrer-dee]
week une semaine [ser-men]
a week today dans huit jours [dōn wee joor]
a week tomorrow/on Monday demain/lundi en huit [der-mān, lān-dee ōn weet]
at the weekend le weekend [wee-kend]
weigh: can you weigh this for me? est-ce que vous pouvez me peser ça? [. . . mer per-zay sah]
weight le poids [pwah]
well: I'm not feeling well je ne me sens pas très bien [jer ner mer sōn pah tray bee-yān]
he's not well il ne va pas bien [eel ner vah pah bee-yān]
very well thanks très bien, merci [tray bee-yān mair-see]
wellingtons des bottes de caoutchouc [bot der kahoo-tshoo]
Welsh gallois [gal-wah]
west l'ouest [oo-est]
West Indies les Antilles [ōn-tee]
wet mouillé [moo-yay]; *(weather)* humide [oo-meed]
wet suit combinaison de plongée [kōnbee-nay-zōn der plōn-jay]

what quel (quelle) [kel]
what is that? qu'est-ce que c'est? [kesker say]
what for? pourquoi? [poor-kwah]
what's that in French? comment est-ce que ça se dit en français? [koh-mont esker sah ser dee on fron-say]
wheel une roue [roo]
when quand [kon]
when is breakfast? à quelle heure est le petit déjeuner? [ah kel err . . .]
where où [oo]
where is . . .? où est . . .? [oo ay]
where is it? où est-ce que c'est? [wesker say]
where can we . . .? où est-ce qu'on peut . . .?
YOU MAY THEN HEAR . . .
près d'ici *nearby*
près de . . . *close to* . . .
très loin *very far*
which quel (quelle) [kel]
which one? lequel (laquelle)? [ler-kel, lah-kel]
YOU MAY THEN HEAR . . .
celui-ci *this one,* celui-là *that one*
whisky un whisky
white blanc [blon]
Whitsun la Pentecôte [pont-koht]
who qui [kee]
wholesale price le prix de gros [pree der groh]
whose: whose is this? à qui est ceci? [ah kee . . .]
why pourquoi [poor-kwah]
why not? pourquoi pas?
YOU MAY HEAR . . .
parce que . . . *because* . . .
wide large [lahrj]
width la largeur [lahr-jerr]
wife: my wife ma femme [fam]
will: will you do it? est-ce que vous pouvez le faire? [esker voo poo-vay ler fair]
I will come back je reviendrai [rerv-yan-dray] *NB: here is the French future tense with the verb 'prendre': je prendrai, il prendra, nous prendrons, vous prendrez, ils prendront; with 'parler': je parlerai etc*
win gagner [gahn-yay]
who won? qui a gagné? [kee ah gahn-yay]
wind le vent [von]

window la fenêtre [fer-naitr]
(of car) la vitre [veetr]
it's in the window c'est dans la vitrine [say do̅n̅ lah vee-treen]
windscreen le pare-brise [par-breez]
windscreen wipers les essuie-glace [ay-swee glahs]
windy: it's too windy il y a trop de vent [eelyah troh der vo̅n̅]
wine du vin [va̅n̅]
wine list la carte des vins [kart day va̅n̅]
red wine du vin rouge [. . . rooj]
white wine du vin blanc [. . . blo̅n̅]
» *TRAVEL TIP: enjoy the simpler 'vins de table' or 'vins de pays': they are generally good quality and cheap*
winter l'hiver [ee-vair]
wire du fil métallique [feel maytah-leek]
(electrical) un fil électrique [. . . aylek-treek]
wish: best wishes meilleurs voeux [may-yerr ver]
(on letter) meilleures pensées [. . . po̅n̅-say]
with avec [ah-vek]
without sans [so̅n̅]
witness un témoin [tay-mwa̅n̅]
will you act as witness for me? est-ce que vous pouvez me servir de témoin? [. . . mer sair-veer . . .]
woman une femme [fam]
wonderful magnifique [mahnee-feek]
wood du bois [bwah]
(forest) un bois
wool de la laine [len]
word un mot [moh]
I don't know that word je ne connais pas ce mot [jer ner koh-nay pah ser moh]
work travailler [travah-yay]
it's not working ça ne marche pas [sah ner marsh pah]
how does it work? comment ça marche?
I work in London je travaille à Londres [jer trah-vie . . .]
worn out usé [oo-zay]
worry les soucis [soo-see]
don't worry ne vous inquiétez pas [ner vooz a̅n̅k-yay-tay pah]

I'm worried about . . . je suis inquiet pour . . . [jer swee ank-yay poor]
worse: it's worse c'est pire [say peer]
he's getting worse son état s'aggrave [son ay-tah sah-grahv]
the worst le pire
worth: it's not worth that much ça ne vaut pas autant [sah ner voh pah oh-ton]
is it worthwhile going to . . .? est-ce que ça vaut la peine d'aller à . . .?
[esker sah voh lah pen dah-lay ah]
50F worth of petrol pour cinquante francs d'essence [poor . . .]
wrap: could you wrap it up? est-ce que vous pouvez me l'envelopper? [. . . mer lonv-loh-pay]
wrench une clé anglaise [klay on-glayz]
wrist le poignet [pwahn-yay]
write écrire [ay-kreer]
could you write it down? est-ce que vous pouvez me l'écrire?
I'll write to you je vous écrirai
[jer vooz aykree-ray]
writing paper du papier à lettres
[pahp-yay ah laitr]
wrong: I think the bill's wrong je crois qu'il y a une erreur dans l'addition [jer krwah keel yah oon ay-rerr don lahdees-yon]
there's something wrong with . . . il y a quelque chose qui ne va pas dans . . . [eelyah kelker-shoz kee ne vah pah don]
sorry, wrong number! excusez-moi, j'ai fait un faux numéro
[exkoo-zay mwah jay fay an foh noomay-roh]
you are wrong vous vous trompez
[voo voo tron-pay]
X-ray une radio [rahd-yoh]
yacht un yacht [yot]
yard
» *TRAVEL TIP: 1 yard = 91.44 cm = 0.91 m*
year une année [ah-nay]
this year cette année
next year l'année prochaine [. . . proh-shain]
yellow jaune [jon]

yes oui [wee]
yesterday hier [yair]
the day before yesterday avant-hier [ahvo͞nt-yair]
yesterday morning/afternoon hier matin/après-midi [. . . mah-ta͞n, ahpray-mee-dee]
yet: is it ready yet? est-ce que c'est déjà prêt? [esker say day-jah pray]
not yet pas encore [pahz o͞n-kor]
yoghurt un yaourt [yah-oort]
you vous [voo]
» *TRAVEL TIP: we have systematically given the more formal 'you' form in this book: the 'vous' form; with friends or young people, you can use the less formal 'tu' form, which sounds the same as the 'je' form: 'je veux', 'tu veux'; for 'your', the less formal form is 'ton, ta, tes'*
young jeune [jern]
your votre, vos [vohtr, voh]
your car/son votre voiture/fils
your tickets/cars vos billets/voitures
it's yours c'est le (la) vôtre
these are yours ce sont les vôtres [ser so͞n lay vohtr]
see **you**
Youth Hostel une auberge de jeunesse [oh-bairj der jer-nes]
» *TRAVEL TIP: you will be asked to produce your YHA card and passport*
zero zéro [zay-roh]
below zero en dessous de zéro [o͞n der-soo . . .]
zip une fermeture éclair [fairmer-toor ay-klair]
zone bleue *area where you can only park for a limited period and must display a parking disc (enquire at the 'syndicat d'initiative')*
zoo le zoo [zoh]

1 un [a̅n̅]
2 deux [der]
3 trois [trwah]
4 quatre [kahtr]
5 cinq [sa̅n̅k]
6 six [sees]
7 sept [set]
8 huit [weet]
9 neuf [nerf]
10 dix [dees]
11 onze [o̅n̅z]
12 douze [dooz]

13 treize [trayz]
14 quatorze [kah-torz]
15 quinze [ka̅n̅z]
16 seize [sayz]
17 dix-sept [dee-set]
18 dix-huit [deez-weet]
19 dix-neuf [deez-nerf]
20 vingt [va̅n̅t]
21 vingt-et-un [va̅n̅-tay-a̅n̅]
22 vingt-deux [va̅n̅t-der]
23 vingt-trois [va̅n̅t-trwah]

30 trente [tro̅n̅t]
40 quarante [kah-ro̅n̅t]
50 cinquante [sa̅n̅-ko̅n̅t]
60 soixante [swah-so̅n̅t]
70 soixante-dix [swah-so̅n̅t-dees]
71 soixante et onze [swah-so̅n̅t ay o̅n̅z]
72 soixante-douze [swah-so̅n̅t dooz]
» *TRAVEL TIP: in Switzerland and Belgium, 'septante'* [sep-tont], *'septante et un' etc*
80 quatre-vingts [kahtrer-va̅n̅]
81 quatre-vingt un [. . . a̅n̅]
90 quatre-vingt-dix [kahtrer-va̅n̅-dees]
91 quatre-vingt-onze [. . . o̅n̅z]
» *TRAVEL TIP: in Switzerland and Belgium, 'nonante'* [ner-nont], *'nonante et un' etc*

100 cent [so̅n̅], **101** cent un [so̅n̅ a̅n̅]
200 deux cents, **285** deux cent quatre-vingt cinq
1000 mille [meel], **2300** deux mille trois cent
1 000 000 un million [mee-yo̅n̅], **0** zéro [zay-roh]
0.5 zéro virgule [veer-gool] cinq, 0,5

1st premier [prerm-yay], **2nd** deuxième [derz-yem]
3rd troisième [trwahz-yem], **21st** vingt-et-unième
[. . . ay-oon-yem], *etc (see also* **date***)*

» *TRAVEL TIP: telephone numbers are read out as two- or three-figure numbers: 220450 is 22/04/50 (vingt-deux/zéro quatre/cinquante); 2240098 is 224/00/98 (deux cent vingt-quatre/zéro zéro/ quatre-vingt-dix-huit)*